# REVIEW

"I wish I'd had this volume when I was in college. It's an essential text for those who are studying psychotherapy and related fields.

"Heussenstamm may become the Siskel and Ebert of psychotherapy."

**Dan Millman**
Author of *Way of the Peaceful Warrior*

"Dr. Heussenstamm offers a creative and entertaining approach to deciphering the psycho-babble that surrounds us. The use of film lends a richness of imagery that gives life to the definitions. Therapists will find this a useful introductory book for their new clients."

**Hyla Cass, M.D.**
Psychiatrist

"Society is inundated with psychological terms. Finally, there is a book for the general public that explains them in a very clear and fun fashion. This truly is an impressive piece of work, combining anecdotal dialogue with insightful descriptions. No library (personal or public) should be without it."

**Andrea Diem**
Professor of Philosophy
Mt. San Antonio College

"Heussenstamm has zeroed in to the heart of psychological insights without the use of psycho-babble. Rather, she has communicated, in down-to-earth terms, an understanding of what has heretofore been the arcane language of psychology. Her unique use of appropriate film titles provides vivid examples of the terminology she is defining."

**Reva T. Frankle, Ed.D., R.D.**
Nutritional Consultant
Weight Watchers International

"A delightful dictionary of psychological terms, with illustrative films. A must ...."

**Judith-Annette Milburn, Ph.D.**
Director, Center for Conscious Living

# BLAME IT ON FREUD

# BLAME IT ON FREUD

## A GUIDE TO
## THE LANGUAGE OF PSYCHOLOGY

**FRANCES K. HEUSSENSTAMM, Ph.D.**

## North Star Publications
Georgetown, Massachusetts

Library of Congress Catalog Card
Number:  93-83263

ISBN Number: 1-880823-02-0

First Printing 1993

Cover design: Tamsen E. George
Editing: John S. Niendorff

North Star Publications
P. O. Box 10
Georgetown, MA  01833

Printed in the United States of America

# ACKNOWLEDGEMENTS

I express my gratitude to:

...John Niendorff, for superb editing;

...George Trim, my publisher, in whose mind the idea for a self-help, psychological reference book was born;

...Marcia Harris, Anna and Frank Harding, and Nancy Sanchez, for reading the manuscript and making valuable suggestions;

...Raemunde Baird; Edith Baumann-Hudson and Lucius Hudson; Janet Bailey-MacKenzie; Gita Breslin; and Paul, Mark, and John Heussenstamm, for naming their favorite movies.


Gratitude for permission to quote from:

Klein, A. *The Healing Power of Humor: Techniques for Getting Through Loss, Setbacks, Upsets, Disappointments, Difficulties, Trials, Tribulations, and All That Not-So-Funny Stuff.* Jeremy Tarcher, Los Angeles. 1989.

Mindess, Harvey. *Laughter and Liberation: Developing Your Sense of Humor.* Nash. 1971.

Moyne, J. and Banks, C. (trans.) *Open Secret: Versions of Rumi.* Threshold. 1984.

# DEDICATION

To M. J., who said with love, "You ought to be writing...."

To B. J., for encouragement and profound insight.

To all the members of my family, with gratitude for what
they've taught me.

# CONTENTS



## PSYCHOLOGICAL TERMS

## APPENDICES

# INTRODUCTION

## *Want to Learn More about People?*

Do psychological words and phrases–sexual abuse, recovery, dependency and co-dependency, addiction, inner child, pervert, anal retentive–either puzzle or annoy you? If they do, I wrote this book for you. It includes many of the terms you probably run into every day–in newspapers and magazines, on TV and radio, while talking with friends.

The material is organized alphabetically, from "Abuse" to "Zest." If you have a question about a particular word, you can turn right to it and find a simple definition. Then comes a brief discussion, and freeze-frames or snapshots of conversations that illustrate it. At the bottom of each page is a list of films you can screen at home using your VCR to learn more about the term.

Why do I call the book *Blame It on Freud*? Because the title is ridiculous! Because Sigmund Freud's theories, which irrevocably changed our way of looking at human beings, raised more questions than they answered. Because his discoveries were momentous, though certain of his theoretical biases continue to lead his followers and critics into violent arguments.

Freud (1856-1939), a Viennese medical doctor whose specialty was neurology or "nervous" diseases, was one of the most influential men of the past two hundred years. He's right up there with Darwin and Einstein. Freud was the first person to recognize that each of us has a mysterious hidden part–a vast ocean of possibilities, memories, dreams–just beneath the surface mind. He named it *the Unconscious^* and he showed us how to access its depths by paying attention to dreams, strange little slips of the tongue, quirky misreadings of people and situations, and mysterious patterns of behavior.*

The immensity of his brilliance can be measured by the sheer number of words in our contemporary vocabulary, and the fields of exploration, that evolved directly from his find: psychiatry; clinical, industrial, personnel, organizational, and social psychology; clinical social work and counseling; psychotherapy; psychometrics (tests and measurement of mental abilities); and psychoanalysis.

Furthermore, his influence is felt in medicine, education, the arts,

---

* *The symbol ^ means I have devoted an entire page to that specific topic, and you can look it up alphabetically.*

human development, engineering, design, advertising and public relations, market research, military and police science. Psychotherapy, humanism, and a growing knowledge of the Unconscious have been among the beneficial effects of Freudian thought.

Freud's limitations? One of them was, most certainly, his inability to recognize the spiritual dimension of human beings. He could not acknowledge that the Unconscious encompasses the transcendent. His theories also led to narcissism,^ irresponsibility, misallocated resources, and the denigration of women. His ideas have touched each one of us, for good or ill.

The work of Carl Jung (1875-1961), a Swiss physician nineteen years younger than Freud, generated other new words I have included. In his youth, Jung (pronounced *Yoong*) joined a circle of Freud's colleagues and admirers. Eventually, however, the two men disagreed about the future of the burgeoning field of psychoanalysis. Jung went his own way, which included the rigorous pursuit of many unconventional paths into the Unconscious.

Why do I suggest you watch motion pictures (movies, films, flicks, videos, the cinema) to learn more about psychology? Watching people in movies and speculating about the motives for their behavior is the next best thing to firsthand experience. If you'll alternate between watching movies and reading about human behavior, you can create your own psychology course at home and build a background of information very rapidly.

For most terms, I found several films to illustrate my definition; each one comes at the subject from a different angle. There is a lot to see in every film, sometimes more than you bargained for. Many of the movies will stretch you. All of them illustrate my points, though I don't tell you what to look for. See for yourself.

Most of these films will be easy to find; others are less readily available. Do you know that videos are free at most public, college, and university libraries? Some of my recommended films are there. To find others, use video stores and purchase catalogues, and scan the TV schedules so you can catch them when they appear on regular television.

Movies illustrate the heroic and the devious in human behavior better than I can do it in words. Films are a voice of the collective–all of us–an art form that belongs to everyone in the twentieth century. Screenwriters, directors, producers, actors, and actresses are among the people who have their fingers on the pulsebeat of humanity.

Films tell and retell the great myths of all time. According to Geoffrey Hill, author of *Illuminating Shadows: The Mythic Power of Film*, going to the movies provides a sacred experience for many people. Today's cinemyths, he notes, are shown in cathedral-like shrines to hushed audiences who have ritual corn in their hands.

Film characters dramatize archetypes^ in the Collective Unconscious.^ You can experience a permanent change in your awareness by involving yourself in a series of films that are mythic in impact. Such films as *Rumble Fish, Taxi Driver, Repo Man*, and *Field of Dreams* show us totally new ways to share the prophetic visions of a writer or director.

## Watch Movies and Learn about People
## at the Same Time

When I see a movie I enjoy the story and cinematography first. But I also pay attention to my feelings. If my feelings are particularly strong, they tell me I have healing to do or unresolved problems to work on. For example, when I find myself crying with a character who has suffered a loss, I know I am weeping about my own losses.

I look for patterns of behavior exhibited by the characters. Does the central character abandon himself or others (perhaps because he was himself abandoned as a child)? Does the central character think of herself as a victim? Is the central character self-destructive? Is the central character unable to love and make a commitment? (See my pages on "anal retentive," "masochism," and "sadism" for examples of other patterns.)

To begin your own journey into the Unconscious and the field of psychology, choose a word or concept and get a film about that subject. When you are ready to watch it, relax and make yourself comfortable. Unplug the telephone so you won't be interrupted or distracted and miss something. Have a journal or some scratch paper handy. If you read my definitions just before you screen the movie, your attention will be more focused and you'll be alert to what to look for. (Sometimes the behavior I want you to catch is obvious, sometimes it is buried or merely implied.)

What if you've already seen a film? See it again. Bring a beginner's mind, an open mind, to a film you have already seen, because you may have been so caught up in the story when you first saw it that you missed some subtle exchanges and interactions between people. If you have enough time when screening a movie you haven't seen before, I recommend you see it twice. The first time for the pleasure of the drama, the second time for serious consideration. Occasionally you may need to see a powerful film several more times, because each viewing progressively peels off layers of your feelings and produces a different impact.

To check your perceptions, invite friends or family (not young kids) to watch with you. The more people, the more varied the perspectives. After you show a film to a group, listen to them talk about it. Sometimes you'll wonder if you all just saw the same film, because everyone's personal perspectives on the world are unique and people see only what they want to see, what they are ready to see. By comparing your observations to theirs, you'll learn more about your own perceptual biases.

A few of these movies are air-head comedies and turkeys, but some are guaranteed to shake your psyche, even shock you. Pay attention to your reactivity–to your feelings during and after the film. What you react to is crucial to understanding yourself and other people.

The more powerful your negative reaction, the closer a film is to difficult material or a darkside^ character in your own Unconscious. The more inspired you feel, the closer a film is to that wonderful part of you, the Ecstatic Deep Self, which responds to the beautiful with the joy of being alive. That part also lives in the Unconscious.

Scenes you remember–whether immediately afterwards or the next day–are loaded with clues about the location of your inner raw edges, hidden issues, unknown wounds, and the sources of your inspiration. Bring your sense of humor even to the darkside films and don't get too serious about any of them. They provide a good opportunity for you to test your ability to center^ or to express repressed^ emotion.

I urge you to keep track of any disturbances and memories which come up. Write in a journal or start a file in your computer. In a separate section, record dreams which follow movie viewing. See if you can identify the same kinds of patterns in your dreams that I'm urging you to look for in films. Your journal will become a custom-tailored, personal record of the currents of emotion in your psyche.

My hope is that you'll find many of these films as fascinating as I have. If you come upon a stimulating or useful movie I missed, I'd be pleased if you'd write me a note about it in care of my publisher.

Frances Heussenstamm, Ph.D.

# BLAME IT ON FREUD

# ABUSE, OF SELF (MASOCHISM^)

*Engaging in self-destructive behavior.*

Self-abuse relieves both psychological conflict and physical tension for a moment, making the self-abuser feel better. Depression usually follows.

**Student:** "Exactly what do you mean by self-abuse?"
**Prof:** "Obvious examples are physical mutilation of your own body, such as self-flagellation or the whipping done by religious fanatics. Less obvious are nail-biting, tearing cuticles until they bleed, and picking scabs. We can add all the compulsive behaviors: compulsive sex with strangers; compulsive shopping, especially with credit cards; compulsive gambling; and the eating disorders–compulsive overeating, forced vomiting, or self-starvation."
**Student:** "What about high-risk sports like bungee-cord jumping and parachute jumping? Or not following doctor's orders, substance abuse, frequent serious injuries and automobile accidents, and smoking?"
**Prof:** "Those are all indirectly suicidal. Killing yourself can be considered the ultimate self-abuse."

**Man:** "When I was a child I was told that masturbation was self-abuse, so I felt guilty and did it anyway. I didn't get warts or grow hair on my hands, and now I know it's normal."
**Therapist:** "It is, unless carried to extremes."

**Fatty:** "What's compulsive overeating?"
**Therapist:** "Using food to stuff down feelings. In a few cases there are physical causes, too. One of them is unbalanced brain chemistry, due either to genetic predisposition or to allergies."

**Wife:** "They say even exercise can be self-abusive, but you know I have to ride my bike every night between 7 and 8!"
**Husband:** "What if the kids get sick?"
**Wife** *(bellowing)*: "They'd better not!"

**Kid joke:** "Why did the moron keep hitting himself in the head?"
**Answer:** "Because it felt so good when he stopped."

*Films: Eating, Fatso, Torchlight, Looking for Mr. Goodbar, La Grand Bouffe, Ironweed, The Gambler.*

# ABUSE, OF OTHERS (SADISM^)

*Taking pleasure from inflicting pain on others.*

Sadists were physically or psychologically brutalized in childhood, and grow up eager to subject others to the same kind of suffering. Sadists must have victims who are either helpless to prevent themselves from being hurt or who seek out pain (masochists^).

Sadistic behavior includes wife-beating, child-molesting, child-neglect, incest, verbal and physical intimidation, torture, rape, pillage, murder, slavery of any kind, abandonment of children and wives, drive-by shootings, gang turf wars.

**Sadistic mother:** "Eat! Every bite! Chew that up!"
**Child** *(gagging)*: "But I'm already full."

**Female client:** "All my facial bones have been broken, and I'm desperate to stop choosing battering men for lovers. Can you help me?"
**Therapist:** "Yes. Women who love violent men were abused in childhood, so they grew up confused. They mistakenly think being hurt is the same thing as being loved."
**Client:** "That's true about me. My mother would report to my father, 'The brat did so-and-so today,' whereupon my father would haul me downstairs to the basement and beat me."
**Therapist:** "Both your mother and father were sadists. Her for directing his violence toward you instead of protecting you and him for obvious reasons. Of course you pick sadistic lovers, because you loved your parents, no matter how cruel they were. This is pattern behavior. You unconsciously recognize the energy – the essence – of your parents when you choose a new man."

**Father Leo Booth:** "... in religious abuse, the highest source of love is used to create guilt, shame, and ultimately self-hate."
**Parishioner:** "Yes, I know. I'm in recovery from the last church I attended."

**Turned-on normal lover:** "Nice candles and brandy!"
Turned-on S-and-M lover lights the brandy and pours it on you.

*Films: Blue Velvet, Jane Eyre, Silence of the Lambs, Dangerous Liaisons, Sleeping with the Enemy, Fort Apache, Fatal Attraction, La Strada.*

# AGING

*The predictable sequence of biological declines that, beginning around age 60 in most people, affect the mind and body.*

**Common proverb:** "You're only as old as you feel."
**Another:** "We grow too soon old and too late smart."
(Two different ways to regard the aging process.)

**Counselor:** "Now that you're over 60, what are your major concerns?"
**Senior:** "Let's see...reviewing my life to find out if I have any wisdom to share. My health, my finances, what to do with my time since I've retired. Loss of clout in my family and in society. Grieving because friends and family members die. Also, I'm trying not to be depressed because the government may run out of money to fund my social security payments."

**Grandmother:** "I had my last love affair at age 75 with a man in his 40s. I only stopped active sex because I was embarrassed to undress in front of my lover when my arthritic fingers couldn't manage my zippers."
**Granddaughter:** "What a role model!"

**80-year-old:** "I'm as interested in sex as I ever was, but I'm having problems with my erections."
**Doctor:** "Anything you can do to increase the circulation to the lower part of your body will help. Before we start talking about shots and implants, I'd recommend more exercise; weight-loss; lowering your cholesterol; no caffeine or nicotine, because they constrict circulation; and the vitamin niacin, a vasodilator, morning and night. Is your wife still as interested as you are?"
**80:** "She's the one who drove me here."

**Male resident of Old Folks' Home:** "Most of the time I like living here, but I do have one serious complaint. About privacy. There isn't any. If I want to make out with my girlfriend, we have to hide in the bushes."
**Amazed grandson:** "You still do it?"

*Films: Cocoon, On Golden Pond, Lost Horizon, Umberto D, The Shameless Old Lady, Folks, The Trip to Bountiful, Driving Miss Daisy.*

# ALCOHOLISM

*A progressive, genetically transmitted disease which, due to physical complications, is terminal.*

Discredited explanations:
...a behavior learned in childhood from watching one or more adult alcoholics in the family cope with life;
...a drug addiction that stems from abuse of what began as a socially acceptable pastime.

**Hospitalized lush:** "I only drink once a month."
**Psychiatrist:** "And you wound up in the hospital again, unconscious. Alcoholics may drink daily, or only on weekends, or once a month. Periodic drunks like you find that once they start drinking, it's almost impossible to stop."
**Lush:** "Don't you dare call me an alcoholic!"
**Psychiatrist:** "Like all practicing alcoholics you use denial to keep yourself from recognizing your condition. I cannot help you as long as you won't face the truth.... You have a terminal disease."

**Alcoholic father:** "Let's have a drink."
**Daughter:** "But you never stop with one drink."

**Mother** *(denying husband's alcoholism)***:** "Don't make any noise. Your father is sick."
**Terrified children:** "Has he been drinking again?"

**Therapist:** "What's the problem?"
**Client:** "I can't seem to hold a job."
**Therapist** *(recognizing familiar story)***:** "Do you drink?"
**Client:** "No. I mean, never during the day."
**Therapist:** "Only at night then? How frequently would you say you're hung over in the morning?"

**Sorority sister:** "We'll serve champagne."
**Wary coed:** "Uh-oh! My mother had a little drinking problem, and I'm afraid to touch the stuff."
**Sis:** "Sparkling cider in a champagne glass looks good, and you won't have to stand around explaining...."
**Coed:** "I'm so glad I told you."

*Films: Days of Wine and Roses; Moon over Parador; The Lost Weekend; Paris, Texas.*

# ALIENATION

*Being estranged from something. When we feel as if we're outsiders in our own family, or that we don't belong in our home town or in our society, we're alienated.*

Severely alienated people feel life is *meaningless*, that they're *powerless*. They can't or won't live by common social rules or norms (*normlessness*), are *socially isolated*, and feel life is *hopeless*. They're alone, often friendless, outcasts.

**Professor:** "Alienated people don't register to vote, or if they happen to register, they don't make it to the polls. They're not involved in conventional community activities, and are usually angry or depressed or unmotivated. They're down on everything, including themselves."
**Student:** "Can whole groups of people feel that way?"
**Prof:** "Yes. For example, African-Americans, whose ancestors did not come here on cruise ships. And, of course, gang members, illegal immigrants, gays, minorities, the poverty-stricken who are undereducated and underemployed. Can you think of others?"
**Student:** "The AIDS-afflicted, prison populations, mental hospital inmates, sexual deviates, such as child-molesters. What a grim list!"

**Teacher:** "You're failing all your classes. Hard to get a decent job without an education."
**Gang member:** "My homeboys'll take care of me."

**HIV-positive male:** "Because I'm gay, society cares nothing about me. Due to homophobia, of course."
**Friend:** "Fear of homosexuals is that powerful?"

**Artist:** "Artists are supposed to be alienated, but it's not true. What I'm trying to do here is make the mysterious, unknown parts of myself visible to me. I can recognize them when they appear on the canvas. That's why I make art."
**Collector:** "What about that artist who urinated on a photo of Jesus crucified, titled it 'Piss Christ', and exhibited it?"
**Artist:** "He's alienated. I'm not."

*Films: The Lonely Passion of Judith Hearne, Ironweed, Look Back in Anger, Mississippi Burning, The Magnificent Ambersons, Tchao Pantin, American Me, Mo' Money.*

# ANAL RETENTIVE

*Persons who are unable to or cannot release their emotions. They may also be chronically tense in the bowels or anus.*

The Freudian explanation for anal retentive persons is that they are stuck at the two-year-old level of psychosexual development due to very invasive toilet training. Their mothers tried so hard to control their children's bowel movements that the children engaged in a power struggle with the parent, holding back feces as a way to exert control over the situation and to keep from feeling devoured. Anals grow up to have difficulty releasing almost everything, even junk.

**Neighbor:** "You've piled up a ton of stuff and I don't mean antiques! There's no room for your family! Why not recycle all these magazines, newspapers, bottles, cans, balls of string, rubber bands, and plastic bags? What about these cartons of clothes?"
**Anal:** "I need them. I may use them someday."

**Sexually frustrated husband:** "You're so tight-assed! Can't you ever surrender?"
**Wife:** "This is as surrendered as I know how to be."

**Adult daughter to mother:** "I just got a call from the sheriff. Your neighbors are complaining about the stink coming from your yard. Just how many cats do you have now?"
**Mother:** "About forty."

**Male** (*looking smug*): "Never can say I'm sorry."
**Girlfriend:** "Why not?"
**Male:** "I feel I'd be letting go of something important."
**Girlfriend:** "Ever think about seeing a therapist?"
**Male:** "And have someone stirring around in all my shit?"

**Anal:** "Unless I add up the check–even if it's only four dollars–I refuse to pay the waiter."
**Girlfriend:** "This is ridiculous!"

**Rich anal** (*limping*): "Cheap running shoes kill my feet."

*Films: The Caine Mutiny, Mr. Skeffington, Terms of Endearment, Mr. and Mrs. Bridge.*

# ANALYSIS, PSYCHOANALYSIS

*A course of treatments invented by Freud ^ to heal unconscious patterns that cause pain and problems.*

Psychoanalysis and other forms of psychotherapy are designed to access material in the Unconscious.^ A patient in analysis may see the analyst as often as five days a week for three or more years. In other forms of psychotherapy,^ the average number of total sessions is about six, though therapy could continue once a week for years, depending on the nature of the problem. The objective of analysis and psychotherapy: to assist the patient to become fully functioning–healthier, happier, more creative, more successful in relationships.

**Woman:** "I want a classical analysis."
**Psychoanalyst:** "That's what you'll get. You'll lie on my couch and engage in 'free association,' pouring out whatever enters your head. I will make interpretations during the hour. My interpretations will help you gain insight and self-understanding."

**Grief-stricken man:** "My analyst died after I'd been in treatment for eight years! We weren't finished!"
**Psychologist:** "This is the worst thing that can happen to a patient in analysis. You've had a terrible loss and you must mourn. But you and I can review how much you learned about yourself during all those years. The purpose of life is to live it."

**Student:** "Aren't there a lot of changes going on in psychoanalytic thinking these days?"
**Professor:** "Yes. Freud was a genius, but he had biases. The feminists, for example, have attacked him for his theory that penis-envy is one of the standard emotional problems of most women."

In *Sleeper*, Woody Allen is quick-frozen and put in cold storage for future revival. Upon being thawed, when his aluminum foil wrap is unrolled as though he's a TV dinner, he asks, "What year is it?" "2173," someone answers. Jubilant, Allen explodes: "By now my analysis would be finished!"

*Films: Freud,* and the documentary film *Boundaries of the Soul: Explorations in Jungian Analysis.*

# ANGER, PERSONAL

*Anger is a self-selected response to injury, insult, or threat. Beneath anger is hurt or fear.*

Researchers speculate that babies, when they are hungry or wet and mother does not come promptly, experience fear, then anger. Discomfort changes to terror and crying is more and more frantic, until the child is hysterical. Exhaustion follows hysteria. If this kind of neglect is frequent and severe, the child can become physically ill (obvious) or mentally ill (not so obvious). The result is an angry, destructive, defiant child or a depressed, withdrawn one.

As we are socialized during childhood, we learn from parents whether or not our anger is acceptable. If it isn't, we suppress it and, in later years, may not even know we are carrying it in our body. When we are angry, adrenalin is pumped into the bloodstream, causing rapid heartbeat and higher blood pressure. Chronic anger, conscious or unconscious, can take a heavy toll on the body and lead to illness.

**Baby** *(crying like crazy for the umpteenth time)*: "I'm hungry, I'm wet, I'm scared!"
**Mom** *(young or immature or sadistic)*: "Later for you."
**Baby** *(furious)*: "I'll get even with you if it's the last thing I ever do."
**Baby** *(exhausted from crying)*: "Life is not worth living."

**Healthy woman** *(angry, barks at guy in crowded subway)*: "You're standing on my feet! Get off!" (He mumbles, "I'm sorry." She cools down and forgets it.)
**Neurotic woman** *(to herself)*: "This guy is standing on my feet on purpose. If only I could think of a way to get even." (She says nothing and exits the subway with a literal pain in her neck or in her guts.)

**Therapist:** "It's too bad the old carpet beater was replaced by a vacuum cleaner. Grandma used to beat the devil out of the throw rugs after fights with Grandpa."

*Films: Network, To Sleep with Anger, Rage, The Duellists, Miss Sadie Thompson, The Godfather, Dances with Wolves.*

# ANGER, COLLECTIVE

*Rage expressed in mob lynchings, riots, revolutions, political upheaval, and wars.*

The Rodney King verdict in Los Angeles triggered insurrection. Toll: 58+ deaths and 1300+ arrests, millions of dollars of property damage.

**Hood #1** *(on the phone during the riots)*: "What channel are you watching?"
**Hood #2:** "Five."
**Hood #1:** "Turn to channel 7. There's a better fire on that one."

**Distraught client:** "What are we to make of genocide, or of these political and military bloodbaths?"
**Therapist:** "When rage rises up out of the Collective Unconscious^ for whatever reason, it shows us the truth about ourselves. Human beings are all born with the capacity to destroy and to create."
**Client:** "I'm supposed to accept all this slaughter?"
**Therapist:** "Not accept but understand more about the nature and potential of each person. First understand, then we can speculate about solutions."

**Conscientious change-agent:** "People are furious about inner-city schools! I feel as if we are in a war zone, working 70 hours a week just to keep the lid on."
**Superintendent:** "We know how angry they are with their children's low achievement. To be able to reform the schools, our response to these attacks has to include enough self-care to avoid burn-out. Do the best you can. No one expects you to finish the work all by yourself. Just do a reasonable part."
**Change-agent:** "In the face of rage, how much is that?"
**Superintendent** *(after a long pause)*: "That's the most difficult question I've ever heard!"

**1860s Native American:** "You think the Indians should just lie down and die because you want to expand the U.S. to the Pacific Ocean?"
**Cavalry officer:** "Yes."

*Films: A Question of Silence, War and Peace, All Quiet on the Western Front, The Young Lions, The Boat (Das Boot), The Deer Hunter, JFK, 12 Angry Men, The Ox-Bow Incident.*

# ANXIETY

*An inescapable sense of dread or fear of impending or approaching danger or disaster when the source or content of that danger is unknown, can't be defined, or has no name (free-floating anxiety).*

Anxiety is extremely painful uneasiness of mind which can cause strangling distress and emotional paralysis. It may have objective causes, such as arriving home late in a high-crime neighborhood, or it may have more subjective causes, such as emotional conflict or repressed impulses–those that are forbidden and pushed down into the Unconscious.^ (See REPRESSION)

**Student:** "What do you mean by 'subjective' anxiety?"
**Professor:** "It's personal. For example, if you were raised to believe sexual impulses are sinful, then any kind of sexual arousal will have to be repressed and can become a source of anxiety."

**Therapist:** "I feel your anxiety comes from being split off from the intuitive part of yourself and trying to make decisions only with facts."
**Uptight client:** "If I don't have all the facts, I worry that I might make a mistake."
**Therapist:** "Worry is only a cover for future anger you don't feel you'll be entitled to have. When you do discover you've screwed up, your pattern is to become angry and attack yourself instead of being compassionate. You hurt yourself instead of learning to say, 'next time....' What you do say is, 'if only,' the deadliest phrase in the English language."

**Therapist** *(to client having an anxiety attack)*: "I am not going to permit you to pace and wring your hands in here. Run up and down the six flights of stairs to my office. That will reduce your anxiety by changing your brain chemistry for the moment, then we can work on your problems."

**Woman:** "I want a baby but I keep having abortions."
**Therapist:** "Do you feel a fetus is a parasitic little vampire in the womb that will devour you?"
**Woman:** "That's it exactly!"

*Films: Betty Blue, Brazil, Don't Look Now, A Woman under the Influence, High Anxiety, Scenes from a Marriage, Dead Calm.*

# APATHY

*Personal: A cover for individual despair. Passivity. A consequence of trauma or disillusion. The opposite of zest.^*
*Collective: A cover for societal despair. Inertia. Disengagement from the political and social processes of society. A result of widespread loss of hope.*

Apathy is one of the characteristics of our era. The only antidote for despair is creativity. Nothing else works.

**Stay-at-home mother:** "I'm hooked on these soaps. I can't seem to get myself going anymore."
**Neighbor:** "Let's start a new business. I've been wanting to get into marketing and I have an idea...."

**Vietnam vet:** "I just went through too much. Fucked myself up with dope, was unwelcome at home, never could get a decent job, and now I don't care anymore."
**Therapist:** "We'll have to get creative to heal your wounds, beginning today!"

**Middle-aged:** "I'm dying of boredom^ with my job. I feel impotent and disempowered in the political process. Who cares if I vote or not?"
**Politician:** "You can make a difference. Get out there and register."
**Middle-aged:** "Why? You pay no attention to my anguish anyway."
**Politician:** "God help us all if you think I don't care. There are so many creative ways you could be loving and serving your community. Won't you even try?"

**Student:** "The fees are going up at college. I already work full time and carry eight units on top of that. I'll never make it. I'm so tired of it all."
**Prof:** "What's your major?"
**Student:** "Sociology."
**Prof:** "Then you must love people very much. It's so important that we show this loving side of ourselves to each other, because the whole species is going through the dark night of the soul."

*Films: It's a Wonderful Life, Gandhi, Cinema Paradiso, Bagdad Cafe, Fried Green Tomatoes, Field of Dreams, Repo Man.*

# ARCHETYPES

*Various aspects of the vast content of the universal Collective Unconscious^ that can also take form in individuals. Mythologic characters.*

Common archetypes, which appear in stories all over the world: the Warrior, the Great Mother, the Universal Father, the Green Man, the Virgin, the Black Madonna, the Lover, the Whore, the Merchant, the Hero, the Villain, the Savior, the Fool, the Victim, the Priest, the Magician, the Witch, the Crone or wise old woman, the Priestess, the Counselor, the Wild Woman, gods and goddesses of all kinds.

**Vietnam vet:** "I don't know what came over me. I just had to go there and fight for America."
**What Carl Jung would say:** "The Warrior archetype is activated in most men whenever there's a war. That would explain it."

**Young mom:** "My world changed when I got pregnant. I felt this overwhelming concern, not only for my coming child, but for all children everywhere."
**Midwife:** "I've seen this happen so often. When the archetype of the Great Mother becomes active, a mother wants to take care of the world."

**Psychology student:** "I've been studying Carl Jung's ideas about archetypes and I think one obvious example is a nun like Mother Teresa...who gives her life for the love of God."
**Prof:** "Yes. Virginal women who sacrificed for others, devoted themselves to a spiritual life, and tended temples and churches have been known throughout history."

**Tourist:** "What's this 'Black Madonna' I've read about?"
**Swiss guide:** "I think she's a secret remnant, left over from the days of the goddess religions in Europe. She dates back to earlier than Christianity."
**Tourist:** "No kidding!"

*Films: Robin Hood, Jesus of Montreal, Iphigenia, The Bad Seed, Pretty Woman, Mean Streets, Raging Bull, The Lair of the White Worm, Never Cry Wolf, Star Wars, Romeo and Juliet, Raiders of the Lost Ark, Nights of Cabiria, Sergeant York, Devi, Black Orpheus, Lawrence of Arabia, Meet John Doe, Shane.*

# ASTONISHMENT

*The capacity to be amazed by something wonderful. Children are born with the capacity for astonishment, and it is found in adults we identify as creative. The opposite of boredom, cynicism, bitterness, and a jaded view of the world.*

One goal of therapy is to restore joyfulness and openness to new ideas.

**Client:** "Is it true that my negative reactions to people can show me the disowned or dark side^ of my Unconscious^?"
**Therapist:** "Yes. It's one of the most effective ways to identify your shadow and eventually to embrace all of yourself."
**Client:** "That's astonishing!"
**Therapist:** "Isn't it a sensational idea? The very people we hate turn out to be great teachers for us...that is, if we are trying to awaken to all of who and what we are. Tell me about a person who disgusts you. Point your finger at him or her, and you'll be revealing the unknown, dark side of yourself."
**Client:** "Let's start with my father...!"

**Art critic:** "I've looked at hundreds of works of art and these paintings of yours are fabulous. When I consider the sheer number of them, I am amazed!"
**Artist:** "Sometimes when I see the forms that appear on the canvas right in front of me, it's hard to believe I actually painted them. It seems to me that something right behind me or just below my awareness is actually painting."

**Bible scholar:** "The God of the Old Testament is nothing less than astonishing. All those miracles...burning bushes, the Red Sea parting...90-year-old Sarah smiling into her apron. If we're made in His image, maybe that's what God wants from us...that we should astonish Him!"

**Twenty-year-old Jean Cocteau:** "I am a poet."
**Impresario Diagalef** *(his mentor)***:** "Astonish me! Astonish me, then I'll know you're a poet."

***Films:*** *Terminator 2: Judgment Day, The Miracle Worker* (1962)*, It's a Wonderful Life, Angel on My Shoulder, Beetlejuice, The Dream Team.*

# BLAME

*Pointing a finger accusingly at someone else. Holding others (often mother, father, husband, government, foreigners) responsible for one's troubles, saying things like, "It's all their fault...."*

Blamers forget that when they judgmentally point a finger at someone else, three fingers on their own hand point back to themselves. They give their power away, remain emotional children, and refuse to grow up. If Christian, they may say, "The devil made me do it."

**Husband:** "I heard you've been cheating on me!"
**Wife:** "It's all your fault. I never should have married you in the first place."

**Guilt-making mother:** "You'll be the death of me."
**Child:** "Why did you have me if you didn't want me? I'm just being a child, not trying to kill you."

**Service Manager:** "... factory problem. Not my fault."

**Husband:** "You aren't raising these kids right."
**Wife:** "Huh?"

**Bankrupt Farmer:** "It's the government's fault for urging farmers to go into debt to increase production."
**Farm Agent:** "...and you're a poor manager."

**Foundering American car manufacturer:** "It's the Japanese government's fault because they subsidize businesses."
**Outraged Public:** "No, it's your fault for not designing affordable cars that get good gas mileage!"
**Manufacturer** *(closing plant and moving to Mexico)*: "You're not a good American if you're not buying American."

**Republicans:** "The Democrats!"

**Congress:** "The President!"

**Savings and Loan depositor:** "The bastards!"

*Films: Pinky, JFK, Bedazzled, The Devils, The Parallax View, Rudy, El Norte, Salvador.*

# BOREDOM

*The feeling that somehow your capacity is not being fully used.*

Before the Industrial Revolution, only the richest people had leisure. Grubbing for a livelihood kept most of the population from ever having to deal with the problem of boredom. Farm families were worn out by their struggle to stay alive, and only the Sabbath provided a time of rest and relief.

**Therapist:** "Once you tap into your creativity, boredom is gone forever."

**Non-bored employee:** "I work for Volvo. My crew and I build each complete car from the ground up and we're never bored like workers on ordinary assembly lines."

**TV-bored husband:** "TV is the bland leading the bland."
**Wife:** "Nevertheless, I'm addicted. If I don't see my soaps every day, I feel withdrawal symptoms."
**Husband:** "Turn off the set and let's make love. Then we can cook up something wonderful for dinner."

**Yawning 10th grader:** "Why don't they ever teach us what we want to know?"
**Equally bored pal:** "Because they never ask us."

**Wife:** "Not tonight. The kids wore me out."
**Husband** (*cursing to himself*): "Again? I need more fun. I'm getting a mistress."

**Hood:** "We haven't shot anyone this week. I'm bored."

**Violence addict:** "In this film, not enough people were killed or maimed...not enough blood. It's boring."

**Rowdy British soccer fan:** "We haven't had a riot lately. I feel the need for bashing to entertain myself."
**Sociologist:** "You enjoy the violence more than the soccer?"
**Rowdy:** "Yeah!"

*Films: Modern Times, Marty, Mr. Hulot's Holiday, Ryan's Daughter, Cat on a Hot Tin Roof, Henry VIII.*

# BRAIN, LEFT (see also: BRAIN, RIGHT)

*The source of verbal, linear, analytic modes of thought.*

There is much overlap between the operations of the two halves of the human brain, but research has lead to the identification of some distinctly different characteristics of each.

**Students:** "Left-brain thinking discards the irrelevant as it zeros in on a target. It converges and focuses."
**Prof:** "That's it. The left brain is digital, rational, and can take things apart step by step then put them all back together again in the same order."
**Student:** "When a mechanic is tearing down an engine, is it the left brain that keeps track of everything?"
**Prof:** "Yes. It plans the time and sequences in which events will happen, and regulates things. It draws conclusions based on facts, deduction, logic. It can also abstract, that is, take a tiny bit of data and generalize from it. For example, once the brain sees that one mammal carries its young in a womb and births them live, it can understand that all other mammals probably do the same thing."
**Student:** "What about the manipulation of symbols?"
**Prof:** "That's a left-brain function, which is why the left brain is where arithmetic and mathematical computations are carried out."
**Student:** "So it's logical and linear."
**Prof:** "Indeed. Carefully developed arguments, where one point logically follows another, are the work of the left brain."
**Student:** "This means that in order to develop into a whole person I need to educate both sides of my brain."

**Pre-school teacher:** "Sort all these blocks, please. Put the red ones in that box, the blue ones in that other box, the yellow ones over here in this box, and the white ones there."
**Four-year-old:** "Oh! I can do that!"

**Very compassionate statistics prof:** "I know some of you are intimidated by the thought of having to learn statistics, so I'm going to begin slowly. This is where you put the decimal point."
**Confident student:** "Aren't you overdoing this anxiety bit?"
**Shaky student:** "I love his approach!"

*Films: The Fiendish Plot of Dr. Fumanchu;* any detective story starring Charlie Chan, Sherlock Holmes, or their peers.

# BRAIN, RIGHT (see also: BRAIN, LEFT)

*The source of intuitive, holistic modes of thought.*

Ancient Greeks believed the gods spoke to human beings through a receptive place in the brain. This probably corresponds to our contemporary understanding that intuition and prophetic vision are processed through the right brain.

**Student:** "Will you explain the current ideas about right-brain functions?"

**Professor:** "The right brain deals with what's fluid and dynamic. It is divergent. That means it can begin at any point and go off in all directions. Many inventors start down one path then go off on several others. The right brain is decidedly nonverbal. It's aware, but it sees objects and things without using words a good deal of the time."

**Student:** "Does that mean it has no sense of time?"

**Prof:** "Apparently so. It's very concrete, relating to the now moment rather than to the future. It puts things together to form gestalts or wholes, so it's holistic. It's inclusive."

**Student:** "And facts and data?"

**Prof:** "Not its province. It requires no facts, as such."

**Student:** "Spatial intelligence must be lodged there."

**Prof:** "Yes. It can see objects in relationship and how things fit together, like the parts of an engine, or a painting, or a skyscraper."

**Student:** "Would you say intuition also springs from the right brain?"

**Prof:** "Definitely. The right brain deals with hunches and feelings. It sees patterns of all kinds and makes insightful leaps. It's nonrational."

**Child:** "I just want to move my brush over the paper and see what happens. I can make clouds my own way."

**Art teacher:** "Of course. If and when you need help, I'll be here."

**Art teacher** (*in beginning drawing class for adults*): "Now that you've grown up, if you want to learn how to draw well, you'll have to get back into your right-brain mode, the way children work."

*Films: The Fountainhead, Lust for Life, Amadeus, Moulin Rouge, Big, The Agony and the Ecstacy, The Moon and Sixpence, Camille Claudel,* any film biography of artists, writers, musicians, poets.

# BRAINWASHING

*Persuasion by propaganda (self-serving deception) or salesmanship (cleverly biased information).*

There are at least two kinds of brainwashing. One is violent, forced indoctrination to make someone give up basic political, social, or religious attitudes and beliefs, and accept rigid or regimented ideas counter to those with which the person began. The second is subtle undermining of traditional social values over a long period of time.

*Violent*–**Korean War P.O.W.** *(weakened by starvation and psychological pounding)*: "Maybe my government is the real enemy."

*Subtle*–**Grandmother:** "When we were growing up we were taught that we should save until we had money to buy things. Cash is king. With cash you can get a better deal, save on the purchase price, never pay interest."
**Granddaughter:** "But I want it now!"
**Grandmother:** "You've been brainwashed by advertising that has undermined your common sense. Being sold on the idea that you can have everything you want at the moment of desire will keep you in debt and dissatisfied all your life."

*Violent*–**Consultant:** "In order to bring your son back from his 'religious' conversion, we have to do reverse brainwashing."
**Father:** "You'll kidnap him from the commune?"
**Consultant:** "Yes, and then work on him until I can break him. Board up the windows in one of your bedrooms and put a lock on the door, so he can't escape once we get him here."

*Subtle*–**Doctor:** "Having a C-section instead of labor will be easier on you and the baby."
**Pregnant:** "But women in my mother's generation simply didn't have C-sections unless there was some sort of crisis during the delivery."
**Doctor:** "Times have changed."
**Pregnant:** "And how much more is your bill going to be?"

*Films: Split Image; Ticket to Heaven; 1984; The Manchurian Candidate; Helter Skelter; Ivan the Terrible, Part One; Ivan the Terrible, Part Two; Rapture; Missing.*

# CENTERING

*A process employed by an individual to restore balance in the midst of crisis or after a hard day at the office (e.g., deep breathing).*
*A technique employed in spiritual development to quiet the mind (e.g., fixing one's gaze on the center of a mandala– a circular painting with a center).*

In the face of bad news or good news, the most centered response would be: "Is that so."

**Distraught mother:** "My daughter tried to commit suicide!  She was saved at the last minute by a friend!"
**Therapist:** "Can you bring yourself back to your center, to calm down?"
**Mother:** "Now, when I have a crisis on my hands?"
**Therapist:** "Yes, right now.  Because when you're hysterical, you can't listen, you won't hear much of what's being said to you, and you'll block any important insights that might come up out of the Unconscious.^ "
**Mother:** "How do I do it?"
**Therapist:** "Start with ten long, slow, deep breaths.  Then we'll talk."

**Screaming kid on the telephone:** "There's a riot here!"
**Father:** "Are you in danger?"
**Kid:** "Everybody is looting and burning stores!"
**Father:** "Then get centered immediately.  Stop holding your breath."
**Kid:** "Okay, okay.  I'm slowing down a bit."
**Father:** "What's your next move?"
**Kid:** "I'm coming right home."
**Father:** "You called me because...."
**Kid:** "I'm scared. I just want you to tell me what to do."
**Father:** "If you remember to center, you can always handle a crisis and take care of yourself."

**Friend to co-worker:** "You seem to be running on empty. Exercising before and after work, and a few minutes of meditation, would center you before you go home."
**Colleague:** "I don't have time for that nonsense."
**Friend:** "That's too bad, because you'll probably die young."

*Films: The Karate Kid; The Karate Kid, Part II; The Karate Kid, Part III; Enter the Dragon.*

# CHILDREN

*Offspring. The natural consequence of sexual intercourse. The next generation, which inherits the dreams and the hatreds of its ancestors.*

To some, children are a joy and a gift from God; to some, a burden; to others, a way to get on welfare.

**Famous lost words:** "I'm telling you kids for the last time...."

**Man:** "I was adopted. My adoptive parents love me but I've always longed to know my birth parents and why they gave me away."
**Therapist:** "Are you in pain about this?"
**Man:** "Yes. I've tried to find them to learn what happened."
**Therapist:** "Once you accept that you may never find out, the pain will lessen."
**Man:** "All I know is that my parents were unmarried. My mother was almost forty. My father was a few years younger."
**Therapist:** "This is a moment in your life when you can discover the true meaning of compassion. Try to imagine the conflicting emotions your parents felt, especially your mother, who carried you under her heart for nine months and knew she couldn't keep you."

**Therapist:** "You're crying...."
**Mother:** "My little boy is dying of leukemia."
**Therapist:** "What a loss! How old is he?"
**Mother:** "Only six."
**Therapist:** "When you have grieved the loss, perhaps you'll be able to celebrate that you had him for six whole years. He's taught you a lot about loving."
**Mother:** "All I want to know is, why me?"
**Therapist:** "Why not you?"

**Grandma** (*at funeral home, looking at dead Grandpa*)**:** "He doesn't look right. He just doesn't look right."
**Six-year-old grandson:** "Of course he doesn't look right. You've never seen him dead before."

*Films: Mandy, Parents, Mask, Kramer vs. Kramer, Stella Dallas, Small Change, The Virgin Spring, Cinema Paradiso, Autumn Sonata, A Child Is Waiting, Children of Hiroshima, My Life as a Dog, The Night of the Shooting Stars, A Hungarian Fairy Tale, The Chosen, Children of Paradise, The Parade, Mon Oncle Antoine, Runaway.*

# CO-DEPENDENCY

*A circumstance in which two or more people are so locked into their relationship that the emotions of each depend on the reactions of the others. They are unable to function as independent human beings.*

Co-dependents grow up in a situation where their self-space is so disrespected, they can't develop a full sense of themselves. They become doormats in the presence of other people's wishes and desires. In co-dependent families, parents and children are fused with each other, enmeshed, and have no personal boundaries. Alcoholics, their mates, and family members are co-dependents.

**Martyrwife:** "Poor me. He's been drinking again!"
**Children:** "How can we fix her? How can we fix him?"

**Alcoholics Anonymous sponsor:** "I support recovering alcoholics once they break through their denial system. The non-drinking family members can then shift attention to themselves and their own development through Al-Anon and Alateen, which are extensions of Alcoholics Anonymous for families."

Co-dependent spouses of compulsive overeaters often undermine their partners' efforts to maintain normal weight.

**Husband:** "Here's a lovely box of chocolates for you."
**Wife:** "But you know I'm a chocoholic and I can eat the whole box in one day!"
**Husband:** "I just want you to be happy." (Meaning: *I just want to be in control of our relationship. As long as you're overeating, you're one-down and I'm one-up.*)

**Father** *(on telephone to drug-abusing son)*: "I'll do anything to get you straightened out...pay for whatever program you want to attend. Will you go and detox?"
**Son** *(with no intention to stop cocaine)*: "Okay. Send money."

*Films: The Sheltering Sky, The Color Purple, A Long Day's Journey into Night, The Corsican Brothers, The Three Musketeers,* and any films starring Laurel and Hardy or Abbott and Costello.

# COMMITMENT

*A pledge, a vow, a promise.*

A commitment to support oneself, both emotionally and financially, is essential to a healthy self-concept in an adult. Commitment to the well-being of all humanity and the planet itself underlies the ecology movement.

**Father:** "You're eighteen. Time to take responsibility for your living expenses. I'll pay tuition."
**Son:** "And I'll get a part-time job."

**Depressed patient:** "I don't care."
**Nurse:** "If you want to get well, you must make a commitment to heal and to cooperate fully with your doctor."

**Daughter** *(coming home to mother)*: "Well, as much as it galls me to say it, you were right. We lived together for eighteen months and he still wouldn't make a commitment to marry me."
**Mother:** "I'm so sorry. You must be very disappointed. Men don't marry what they can have so easily, and the basic reason they marry is for regular sex. If women give it away, why should men marry them?"

**Training therapist:** "A therapist's first commitment is to healing... beginning with self."
**Trainee:** "I'm committed to being a healer, but I'm not sure I understand having to heal myself first?"
**Therapist:** "Healers become healers to give others what they, themselves, need. Beginning therapists must know themselves thoroughly and be able to tell the difference between their own wounds and their clients' wounds. That's the commitment!"

**Pilot:** "After all these years of atheism, I discovered I have a deep commitment to the God of my childhood. When we lost that engine and I thought we were all going to die, I prayed."
**Co-pilot:** "Ain't it the truth!"

*Films: Gallipoli, Breaker Morant, Dark Victory, The Black Robe, She Wore a Yellow Ribbon, Stand and Deliver, And the Children Shall Lead, The Miracle Worker (1962), The Mighty Pawns, Gryphon, The Citadel, Breaking Away.*

# COMPASSION

*"Compassion," according to the Dalai Lama, is "the mutual perception of shared weakness." It is the ability to put yourself in someone else's place; to see that your own faults have the same weight as theirs, that you and they are not separate, but are part of the seamless web of all life.*

When we are compassionate, we apologize quickly if we make a mistake or hurt someone. We see that much of our own and other people's behavior is simply the suchness of life. We stop being judgmental.

Rumi, a Sufi mystic (1207-1273 A.D.), said that lost others are not outside of us in the world but, rather, are inside of us.

. . .

Stretch your arms and take hold of the cloth of your clothes
with both hands. The cure for pain is in the pain.
Good and bad are mixed. If you don't have both,
you don't belong with us.

When one of us gets lost, is not here, he must be inside us.
There's no place like that anywhere in the world.

**Client** *(sighing with relief)*: "After hating my mother all my life, I finally see that I'm carrying her same psychological patterns. I feel compassion for both of us."

**W. Brugh Joy, M.D.:** "Compassion is allowing people to be exactly the way they are and exactly the way they are not."

In defending a whore from the mob that wanted to stone her to death, Jesus is quoted in the Bible: "He that is without sin among you, let him first cast a stone...."

**Raped woman** *(after a lot of hard work in therapy)*: "Instead of feeling sorry for myself, I feel compassion. Now I understand what you meant when you said I had a choice about whether I wanted to stay in victim-consciousness^ or really heal myself."
**Therapist:** "You've come a long way, baby."

*Films: Mother Teresa; Stanley & Livingstone; City of Joy; Children of a Lesser God; The Story of Helen Keller; My Left Foot; Brother Sun, Sister Moon.*

# COMPULSIONS

*Compulsions are urges, coming from the Unconscious,^ to perform acts over and over again that are essentially meaningless. Compulsions involve repetitive rituals or repetitive checking, cleaning, ordering, counting, sorting, collecting.*

Compulsive behavior keeps the lid on a garbage can full of rage or fear or both. Such repetitive acts relieve intolerable inner pressure. Compulsive people are always trying to make themselves feel better.

**Client:** "When I come home from running any kind of errand, I have to go straight into my bedroom, take out all my sweaters, unfold and refold them, then put them away again before I can do anything else around the house. It doesn't matter if the ice cream is melting in a shopping bag out in the car."
**Therapist:** "What are you afraid will happen if you don't do that?"
**Client:** "I'll go crazy."
**Therapist:** "You're suffering from OCD–obsessive-compulsive disorder–and behavior-modification therapy can help you."

**Woman:** "I have to scrub the kitchen floor with a toothbrush."
**Psychiatrist:** "Let's do a series of diagnostic checklists. Sounds like OCD to me."

**Compulsive:** "I was meeting my date at the restaurant at 7:30 p.m. I arrived early, so I went to the men's room to comb my hair."
**Friend:** "What happened?"
**Compulsive:** "When I came out to look for her, it was 2 a.m. I don't understand why she didn't wait for me."
**Friend:** "Six and a half hours of hair combing?"

**Nun:** "The evening prayers take about two hours. Every time I make a mistake, I have to go back to the beginning and start over. I'm seven years behind in my prayers at the moment."
**Mother Superior:** "Sister, I'd like you to see a therapist."

**Compulsive:** "All ten of my credit cards are full. I'm $75,000 in debt."
**Credit counselor:** "Hand me your credit cards and watch me cut them up. Next, we'll make a plan to deal with creditors."

***Films:*** *Dead Ringers, The Blue Angel, Ossessione, Obsession, Irezumi (Spirit of Tattoo).*

# CONFLICT

*Tension, frustration, anxiety, and stress that occur when we are grappling with impulses, ideas, or wishes that are in opposition to our fundamental beliefs. Or, indecisiveness in the face of two or more opposing impulses.*

When we have two conflicting impulses, Freudian psychology suggests that the forbidden or least desirable impulse is often repressed.^

**Wife:** "Today I heard an awful thing...that an erect penis has no conscience. That's terrible."
**Husband:** "Get real. What do you think keeps humanity reproducing? Don't you understand that their biology makes men interested in women's bodies?"
**Wife:** "But the commandment against adultery...?"
**Husband:** "A married man is often in conflict. But I'm like all faithful husbands. I recommit to you and our marriage every time I make love to you."

**Father:** "Don't put the boys down that way. You don't understand how to raise men. If you keep nagging, they'll grow up without any balls at all."
**Mother:** "Look who's talking."
**Father:** "That hurt."

**Career woman:** "I want to have a great career, a great marriage, and to raise great children."
**Therapist:** "That's damn near impossible! You'll sacrifice either your health, your husband, your children's well-being, or your job. The big 'S' on those Superwoman T-shirts stands for 'stupid,' 'slave,' or 'sucker.' Take your choice."
**Woman:** "I don't want to hear this!"
**Therapist:** "Look! You're the one who came in today with these unrealistic expectations and the pain they cause."

**Mother** *(sitting down to family dinner)***:** "I really love you kids a lot, but if any one of you spills your milk again tonight, you're dead."

*Films: The Last Detail, The Man with Two Brains, Manhattan, Silkwood, Falling in Love, Heartburn, A New Leaf, The War of the Roses, The Rocky Horror Picture Show, Catch-22, Wrong Is Right.*

# CONSCIOUSNESS

*Scientific definition: a unique inner process in each living organism. Popular definition: personal awareness. The way people experience thoughts, images, sensations, feelings, events from their own insides.*

Consciousness is mysterious and it has been evolving...from "fight or flight" responses when a sabre-toothed cat was about to spring, to the ooh's and aah's we make when we see the latest fuel injected automobile engine or a Fabergé enamelled egg in a museum.

**Client:** "I've totalled four cars."
**Therapist:** "Why are you trying to kill yourself?"
**Client:** "Who me?"

**Amazed:** "Looking for happiness, I married three times. Now I see that I married the same person each time; they just have different names and faces!"
**Therapist:** "That insight is an important part of your development. The more aware you are, the better choices you'll make in every part of your life. That discovery signals an end to sleepwalking."

**Priest:** "To quote Jung,^ 'When an inner situation is not made conscious, it happens outside, as fate. When the individual does not become conscious of his inner contradictions, the world must...act out the conflict and be torn into opposite halves.' "
**Parishioner:** "What does he mean?"
**Priest:** "He means that what happens outside and around us is a reflection of what exists inside of us. We need to discover our inner motives, our inner scripts, our unconscious patterns, and do the necessary work to become more and more awake. Each time we have an insight, it adds to cumulative consciousness...."
**Parishioner:** "... of the whole planet?"
**Priest:** "That's what Jung said."

**Smart-ass kid:** "Why'd you call me to the office again?"
**Counselor:** "You've got an attitude problem."
**Kid:** "Just because I told the teacher she could kiss my butt?"

*Films: It's a Wonderful Life, You Can't Take It With You, Who's Life Is It Anyway?, My Dinner with Andre, Lost Horizon, Angel on My Shoulder, Meetings with Remarkable Men.*

# CONSCIOUSNESS, ALTERED STATE OF

*A change, voluntary or involuntary, from our normal, everyday personal awareness.*

Common ways of altering consciousness include: vigorous exercise, meditation, music, sex, hypnosis, and drugs. With drugs, the side-effects may be unanticipated (alcohol, prescription downers and uppers, tranquilizers, amphetamines, anti-psychotics, anti-depressants).

**Student:** "There are household drugs–like the caffeine in coffee, tea, chocolate, and colas–that have the same narcotic effect as airplane-glue fumes, according to a pamphlet I read."
**Teacher:** "Yes. And street drugs alter consciousness, too. Let's identify them...."
**Student:** "Marijuana, LSD, PCP or angel dust, heroin, crack or cocaine. Designer drugs...like Ecstacy."
**Teacher:** "What about out-of-body phenomena in a near-death experience, when an individual sees himself leaving his body and floating away, then comes back and is revived? Even though we don't understand them yet, do you think they belong on our list of altered states?"
**Student:** "Yes, I do. And here's another challenging one. Remote viewing. Extensive experimenting by the Russian military convinced them that certain clairvoyant individuals can see distant military installations."
**Teacher:** "Okay. And those Hindu exercises to awaken an internal energy they call the 'Kundalini' and progressively raise it to higher levels in the body. Westerners using their techniques have experienced visions, clairvoyance, and even brief episodes of catatonia, which is awakening in the morning and then being unable to move for a few minutes."
**Another student:** "In my church we practice the laying-on-of-hands. The minister induces a trance in himself before doing healing rituals in the name of Jesus."
**Teacher:** "What do you think about seeing auras, the energy fields that surround the human body?"
**Student:** "If I started seeing strange things, I'd think I was going crazy and would want to talk to a doctor."

*Films: Resurrection, The Lawnmower Man, Altered States.*

# CONTROL

*The ability to discipline yourself to reach your objectives after goal-setting and also to release yourself emotionally and physically when it is appropriate. A sense of well-being, competence, creativity, high energy, and presence; the ability to cope (to be cool under fire).*

**Tradition:** "Children should be seen and not heard."
**Jung :** "The urge and compulsion to self-realization is a law of nature, and thus of invincible power...."

The way parents, mentors, and role models control children's natural exuberance powerfully influences the children's feelings of well-being and their ability to control themselves, to be creative, and to take responsibility for their actions. The child-rearing dilemma remains: how to teach children self-control and maintain their "invincible power" to realize their creative potential.

**Interviewer from Fortune Magazine:** "We're doing a study of the differences between outstanding CEOs in the country and those who are just doing okay. How do you account for your extraordinary success?"
**Top CEO:** "No matter how busy I am, I set aside the same hour every day to relax and think about company problems. My secretary holds all calls. Absolutely no one can get to me."
**Interviewer:** "That's it?"
**CEO:** "Yes. I'm in control of my time and space, otherwise I can't think clearly."

**Therapist** *(counseling a couple)***:** "Your power struggles are subtle; nevertheless, your effort to control each other repeats a pattern both of you began as children."
**Wife:** "My mother had no discipline whatsoever. She had two addictions and spent her life trying to control me."
**Therapist:** "That would indicate internal chaos."
**Husband:** "My father was the same way."
**Therapist:** "So you're living your parents' marriages."

*Films: Henry V; A Woman Called Golda; Sunrise at Campobello; The Lady with a Lamp; Norma Rae; Chariots of Fire; My Brilliant Career; All That Money Can Buy; Good Morning, Vietnam; The World According to Garp; The Ballad of Cable Hogue.*

# CREATIVITY

*The ability to give birth to something astonishing.*

Characteristics of highly creative adults: *persistence, tolerance for ambiguity* (able to hold two or more conflicting ideas in mind at the same time), *curiosity, flexibility* (able to look at an idea from more than one point of view and follow it in new directions), *fluency* (able to produce many ideas), *enthusiasm, spontaneity.*

**Prof:** "The irony of our existence is that each animal species feeds on other forms of life in order to maintain itself."
**Student:** "Does that mean something always has to be destroyed for life to continue?"
**Prof:** "Yes. Destruction is an integral part of life and makes the creation of new life possible."

**Designer:** "When we try to improve a machine tool, we play Engineering Bingo all the time. We ask ourselves, 'Can we make it smaller? Turn it sideways, upside-down, or inside out? Stack it? Compress it? Expand it? Double it? Triple it? Combine it?' "

**Mother:** "My young children are endlessly inventive. Human beings come with a built-in ability to manipulate their environment and the objects in it in a creative way."
**Principal:** "I always ask my teachers for ideas about how we, as educators, can evoke our own creative potential to help keep alive the freshness our children are born with."

**Teacher:** "Here are the rules I want you to follow."
**Creative child** *(seeing other possibilities, blurts out)***:** "Why do we have to do it that way?"
**Rigid teacher:** "Because I say so!"
**Creative teacher:** "Do you have another idea?"

**Smart managers to employees:** "We'll reward you with a cash percentage for every suggestion that will either save money or make money for the company."
**Creative employees:** "Have we got ideas for you!"

*Films: The Titan, Edison the Man, The Story of Alexander Graham Bell, Rembrandt, The Fountainhead, Amadeus, The Winds of Kitty Hawk, Vincent.*

# CRISIS

*In Chinese, the two characters that, together, translate as "crisis" represent the words "dangerous" and "opportunity."*

Many people, stuck in ruts and unhappy about it, want to change their lives but don't know how or are afraid of the unknown consequences. However if they create a crisis, or are caught up in one, the energy it generates can get them going in a new direction.

**Screaming husband:** "You left your journal open on the desk, and now I know you've been having an affair for the last two years!"
**Wife:** "I want a divorce!"

**Doctor:** "It's a breast cancer but we caught it in time. You'll have surgery immediately."
**Shocked:** "Am I going to lose my whole breast?"
**Doctor:** "No. We'll do a lumpectomy. Afterward, you'll need to get lots of rest and you're off all fat foods from here on out."
**Shocked** *(a year later)***:** "I used cancer to change my life and it turned out to be a great teacher for me."

**Man:** "I got my two-week notice today. The plant's closing. I'm out of a job!"
**Wife:** "Oh! What a break! You know you hated that job! We'll move south to Galveston and find new jobs. I like swimming in warm water."
**Man:** "What an attitude! Start packing. We'll have a garage sale and get rid of everything we don't want."

**Surfer:** "You're pregnant?"
**Girlfriend:** "Yes. Let's have a baby together."
**Surfer:** "Cowabonga! Me, a father! I'll need a job and place to live. I'll only be able to go surfing on the weekends. You need a doctor. We have to tell my folks and your folks.... Wow! Am I excited!"
**Girlfriend:** "We'll start with my folks."
**Surfer:** "No. Let's go to a surf shop. I want to buy him a boogie board."

*Films: Blade Runner, The Turning Point, Never Cry Wolf, Rain Man, On the Beach, The Medicine Man, Koyaanisqatsi, The China Syndrome, Soylent Green, Dances with Wolves.*

# DARK SIDE, COLLECTIVE

*The source of destructive forces attributed by Christians to the devil and, paradoxically, by Hindus to sacred and holy Shiva: the Destroyer. All cultures have religious or mythological ways to account for plagues, violence, death, and decimation by hurricanes, earthquake, war.*

The collective dark side can be recognized in all the dirty deeds in history that precipitate vast change. Collective darkside thought: "The ends justify the means."

The collective dark side of humanity includes our potential to turn other people into slaves, to wage war and bomb civilians, to feel nothing about mass starvation and injustice, to persecute people whose skin color is different from ours, to pollute the planet, and to support corrupt dictators for purposes of political expediency.

**Early Americans:** "We're not only having slaves, but we're having all of North America, no matter how many Indians we have to kill."

**Spaniards and Portuguese:** "We're having all of Central and South America...."

**Australians:** "We're having all of Tasmania, no matter how many Aboriginals...."

**Communists:** "We're collectivizing all of Russia, no matter how many peasants...." (10,000,000+ died)

**Nazis:** "We're having all of Europe, no matter how many people...." (13,000,000+ died)

**Japanese:** "We're having all of the South Pacific...."

**Khmer Rouge:** "We're having Kampuchea...."

**International cartel CEO** *(looking at a world map and humming)*: "You belong to me...."

*Films: Little Big Man; Roots; Apocalypse Now; The Sky Above, The Mud Below; Santa Sangre; Paths of Glory; Hiroshima: Out of the Ashes; Holocaust; Dr. Strangelove; Viridiana; The Wicker Man; The Klansman; Rapture.*

# DARK SIDE, PERSONAL

*Secret parts of ourselves we are ashamed of. A source of energy for creativity. Anything that comes up in dreams as monstrous, filthy, murderous, or terrifying shows us our dark side.*

Me murder? Oh, yes. I would have killed anyone who threatened my children. There is an "unspeakable" pattern here: a loving mother also has the capacity to commit murder. Jung^ called it the shadow. With most mothers, this point is hard to accept because it conflicts with their images of themselves as self-sacrificing saints.

**Prof:** "Great love has great cruelty as its dark side. Even very loving men and women have to accept their capacity for great cruelty. They have to learn compassion for themselves instead of loathing themselves for it."
**Student:** "The dark side must be a power source in the psyche."
**Prof:** "That's right, it is. As we mature, we learn that what we are ashamed of in our dark side can teach us the greatest lesson of life–compassion."
**Student:** "Are you saying a saint carries, as the shadow, the pattern of a sinner?"
**Prof:** "Yes. These mysterious shadow patterns show up in behavior we can identify if we know what to look for. In the film *Thelma & Louise*, we are puzzled when Louise kills a would-be rapist, even though he is no longer a threat. When we learn she was once a victim, we understand why she's capable of being a victimizer. That's how the killer in her emerged."
**Student:** "What other examples can you give me?"
**Prof:** "Casanovas seduce women and then disappear. Their darkside pattern is seduction/rejection in the service of ego-enhancement. When Jews pass for Christians or light-skinned blacks pass for whites, the darkside pattern is self-hatred/self-rejection, with the flip-side showing up as self-abuse and overcompensating behavior like workaholism."
**Student:** "Would the dark side of nurturing and caretaking be the capacity to kill?"
**Prof:** "Yes. However, to most healers, this is shocking news and they would deny it."

*Films: Prizzi's Honor; Insignificance; The Unbearable Lightness of Being; Body Heat; The Seventh Seal; Suddenly, Last Summer; The Cook, The Thief, His Wife, & Her Lover.*

# DARK SIDE, FEMININE

*The destructive, violent part of women that men are afraid of. The part that has the power to take life instead of nurturing it, and to drive other people crazy.*

Beginning in childhood, with fairy tales like "Hansel and Gretel," "Snow White and the Seven Dwarfs," and "Cinderella," we all learn to be in awe of hostile old ladies and stepmothers. America was founded by Puritans who were so afraid of old ladies that they staged those witch-burning rituals in Salem.

**Prof:** "Almost every culture has dark feminine goddesses or witches. In Bali, she's the witch Ragna, who kidnaps children. In India and Tibet, she's the many-armed goddess of destruction, Kali, the beloved and feared Ma Durga."

**Student:** "One example of the dark feminine in action is an emasculating mother saying to her pre-school son, 'If you don't stop touching yourself there, I'm going to cut it off.'"

**Mother** *(to normal 14-year-old son)***:** "Those girls who go to your school are all sluts and whores. You can tell because they wear make-up. Don't you have anything to do with those girls. They'll give you AIDS, syphilis, gonorrhea, herpes, genital warts, and God-only-knows what else!"

**Husband:** "I'm shocked and disappointed. You've been unspeakably cruel. The kid is only ten, and you burned all his baseball cards because he talked back to you! What did he say?"

**Wife:** "The specifics aren't important. I'm going to break his will if it's the last thing I ever do!"

**Man:** "I'm afraid of being devoured by the feminine. After all, it is the sperm that disappears into the egg at the moment of conception–after its tail falls off!"

**Buddy:** "When I was a kid, my uncle told me that women have teeth in their vaginas."

*Films: The Fourth Man, The Grifters, The Damned, A Question of Silence, The Little Shop of Horrors, The Postman Always Rings Twice, Black Widow, Excalibur, Sunset Boulevard, Diabolique, The Graduate, Mortal Thoughts, Rapture, What Ever Happened to Baby Jane?*

# DARK SIDE, MASCULINE

*The destructive, violent, insidious part of men that women are afraid of. The part that can torture and kill. The opposite of giving life through insemination.*

The images of villainous men in films stir the Unconscious because they are close to our own disowned, darkside material. They cause us to squirm when we compare ourselves with them. "Like the hero, not like the villain." Sometimes, it's the other way around.

**Pimp to his whore:** "You're working for me now and you'd better not hold out, or I'll cut you."

**Enthusiastic gang member** *(watching* American Me*):* "Wow! Did you see the way they all stabbed him at once?"

**Dr. Frankenstein:** "It's alive! It's alive!"
**Frightened:** "That man is evil incarnate."

**Battered woman:** "When he left this morning he told me if I went out of the house today or made any phone calls, he'd break my other arm and beat up the children."
**Therapist:** "Good that you brought them to the shelter. But why today? He's thrashed you before."
**Battered:** "After each beating, he was always sorry and we'd have sex."
**Therapist:** "And this time?"
**Battered:** "I decided sex isn't worth what I have to go through to get it."

**General:** "Let's declare war."
**Aide-de-camp:** "Using what excuse?"
**General:** "Anything. We've got to have those appropriations."

**Police Officer:** "So far we've dug up six bodies ..."
**Killer:** "Only six? Keep looking."

*Films: Sophie's Choice, Angel Heart, M, Ruthless People, The Godfather, Cruising, Dark Forces, Apartment Zero, A Clockwork Orange, Laura, Straw Dogs, Scarface, The Collector, The Sailor Who Fell from Grace with the Sea.*

# DEATH

*"The final stage of growth."– Elisabeth Kubler-Ross*

Death gives meaning to human existence, though few people want to talk about it. To Hindus and Buddhists, death marks only the end of this life and is the start of the next incarnation. To Christians, it is the beginning of life in heaven or hell. Jews, Jains, Muslims, and Zoroastrians all have their own points of view.

**Client:** "I feel a lot of conflict. I know I'm going to die someday, but I don't want to think about it."
**Therapist:** "If we live with 'death on our shoulders,' regarding it as a friend and counselor, we can be grateful for each day and not depressed about the fact that no one gets out of here alive. Death is a problem, but facing problems accelerates maturation."

**Vietnam vet:** "When my best friend was shot and killed right next to me, I had a horrible thought: 'Better him than me.' Now I feel terribly guilty about it."
**Therapist:** "That thought is a normal, but usually unspeakable response to another's death. From the number of people I've talked with who can admit they're glad they are not the body lying in a coffin at the funeral they're attending, I would say you had a universal reaction and have nothing to feel guilty about. Shocked at yourself perhaps, but showing you're human."

**Minister** *(after funeral)*: "Funerals encourage family unity because they bring a clan together to heal any old pain while the family members comfort one another about this new pain. Feuds are set aside and genuine healing can occur."
**Mourner:** "The best funeral I ever attended was arranged by a friend for her lover. At her home, we sat in a large circle, drinking wine and munching. One after another, we took turns telling funny stories about the deceased. We laughed until tears rolled down our faces, recalling the joy we felt from having known him."

"It's not that I'm afraid to die. I just don't want to be there when it happens."–Woody Allen

***Films:*** *Passed Away, Ikiru, May Fools, Harold and Maude, The Loved One, Cries and Whispers, The Seventh Seal, Steel Magnolias, Three Brothers, Flatliners, All That Jazz.*

# DEFENSES

*Personal responses or postures we develop to protect our sensitive and tender inner children, our vulnerability, our sacred cows, the most tightly guarded core of our being. Our defenses may be healthy, appropriate, and useful, or debilitating.*

*Denial:^* You've heard the expression, "Don't confuse me with the facts; my mind is already made up."

*Projection:^* The person we love does not really exist. Instead, he or she is a screen on which we project our idealized images of what is loveable.

*Repression:^* Unconsciously pushing down (into the Unconscious^) or conveniently forgetting unacceptable motives, sexual appetites, terrifying experiences.

*Suppression:* The same as "repression" except the process is done consciously.

*Sublimation:^* Converting the procreative urge into the creative (i.e., sports or art instead of sex).

*Regression:^* Going backward to earlier stages of development (child forgets toilet training when baby brother is born).

*Displacement:^* Redirecting unacceptable feelings (venting hostile feelings on the dog instead of the boss).

*Reaction formation:^* Doing the opposite of what is really felt (mother who hates her child showers it with attention).

*Rationalization^ (or cynicism):* Making up excuses or explanations for negative events, feelings, thoughts. (The fox who couldn't reach the grapes said, "I didn't want them anyway. They were sour.")

*Minimalization (a variation of rationalizing):* "He only gave me a little shove. I'm the one who fell over and broke the glass on the coffee table."

***Films:** Batman, Rebel Without a Cause, I'm Dancing As Fast As I Can, From Here to Eternity, Other People's Money.*

# DELUSIONS

*False, irrational beliefs that have no basis in reality and are maintained even in the face of overwhelming evidence to the contrary. If they are extreme, we call them insane delusions.*

A delusion is an identifying symptom of mental illness. Ordinary, normal people can sometimes be deluded as well, but the delusion passes when the individual has to face reality. The mentally ill person has escaped reality and lives within the delusion.

**Prof:** "Give me some examples of delusion."
**Student:** "Delusions of grandeur, or self-inflation. When a patient says, 'I'm Jesus,' he's deluded."
**Prof:** "What about delusions of persecution?"
**Student:** "A patient might say, 'They're coming to take me away,' or, 'Everyone is out to get me.' "
**Prof:** "And delusions of sin or guilt?"
**Student:** " 'I am responsible for all the evil in the world. I brought it in when I was born.' "
**Prof:** "What about delusions of control?"
**Student:** "That might sound like, 'People are using electricity to tamper with my mind. I'm being short-circuited' or 'My ideas are being broadcast on the airwaves right now' or 'Someone is putting their thoughts in my head.' "
**Prof:** "Good work!"

**Schizophrenic:** "Voices are coming out of my cake mixer."
**Psychologist:** "What do they say?"
**Schizy:** "They're telling me to kill myself."
**Psychologist:** "I'm going to have you see the medical doctor to be put on medication that will stop the voices. Until the medication takes effect, I want you to write down everything the voices say, and bring your journal in to read it to me."

**Beautician** *(to 56-year-old woman)*: "You think you'll look good in that hairstyle? The girl in the picture is only a teenager."
**Deluded:** "It's me all right!"
**Beautician** *(to herself)*: "Oi!"

*Films: The Ruling Class, The Stunt Man, F/X, The Fisher King, The Treasure of the Sierra Madre, Greed, Delusion, Brazil, Hour of the Wolf.*

# DENIAL (A DEFENSE)

*A refusal to face the truth in a situation.*

**Mother** *(upon being told her child was caught using drugs in the restroom at school)*: "No way. Not my kid!" (Accepting this bad news would shatter her self-concept about being a good mother.)
**Observing friend:** "You must be a reincarnation of Cleopatra, the queen of denial!"

**Teenage girl** *(upon being told she's pregnant)*: "But I never had sex."
**Nurse:** "Sure, and a star is shining in the east."

**Accusing father:** "My wallet was on the table. I know exactly how much money I had. There's twenty dollars missing."
**Heroin-addicted son:** "I never touch your money."

**Smoker:** "Lung cancer? Not me."

**Alcoholic:** "I'm a good driver, even when I've had a few drinks, and I am not an alcoholic."

**Compulsive overeater:** "One more doughnut won't hurt."

**Bungee-cord jumper:** "These things never break."

**Couch potato:** "I'll start exercising tomorrow. I can always catch up."

**Promiscuous:** "AIDS? Not me."

**Mistress:** "He'll leave his wife and marry me someday."

**Ditzy:** "$2.99 is less than $3.00."

**Unconscious:** "It won't cost any more if I put it on a credit card."

*Films: Twice in a Lifetime, I Never Sang For My Father, The Trip to Bountiful, Year of the Quiet Sun, Birdy, Mr. and Mrs. Bridge, The Apartment, Crossing Delancey, Alexander's Ragtime Band, Brief Encounter, A Midsummer Night's Dream.*

# DEPENDENCY

*An infantile desire to be taken care of. A major developmental problem in adults. We all need each other for the survival of the human race, but that is mature, collective interdependence, not infantile, individual dependency.*

A baby is attached to its mother by an umbilical cord. Step one toward independence is having that cord cut at birth. Being weaned from the breast and learning to drink from a cup is step two. However, some adults never get past their longing for the breast. Maturation can also be arrested when mother or father deliberately withhold permission to act independently.

**Mother:** "No, you can't go to the store by yourself. You're only ten years old." (All the other kids on the block have been going since they were five.)

**Mother to son:** "If you leave me to marry that girl, I'll never forgive you."
**Independent son:** "Too bad, Mother. I'm getting married anyway."
**Dependent son:** "Yes, Mother."

**Father to daughter:** "No man will ever be good enough for you, especially that flake you're dating now."
**Dependent:** "Will you cut off my allowance if I continue to see him?"

In marriage, when there are dependency and control^ issues, the dialogue may go like this:
**Wife to husband:** "I need to go to the store."
**Husband:** "I'll drive you."
**Wife:** "Won't you ever let me learn how to drive so I can go by myself?"

**Alcoholic:** "I feel nervous. Maybe I'll just have a glass or two of wine."
**Co-dependent^ overweight wife:** "And I'll make a batch of cookies."

**Batterer to ex-wife:** "I can't live without you."
**Wife in recovery:** "Try."

*Films: Now, Voyager; Radio Days; Midnight Express; Where's Poppa?*

39

# DEPRESSION (NOT GRIEF)

*A dysfunctional defense and not the same as grief. A mental/physical condition that may have organic causes, such as a reaction to drugs or disease, or may result from genetic predisposition. If our parents or grandparents suffered from depression, we may inherit the tendency.*

A "presenting problem" is what clients walk into a therapist's office to discuss. The number one presenting problem in America today is depression. Before starting psychotherapy for depression, one should have a physical exam to eliminate the possibility that the depression has been brought on by illness, such as kidney disease, or as a side-effect of prescription drugs.

To a guilt-stricken person, depression is a self-imposed jail sentence. To others, depression is rage turned on the self.

**Therapist:** "Your symptoms are apathy, anger, anxiety, fatigue, insomnia, agitated behavior, and reduced ability to function. You're depressed."
**Male client:** "It's like trying to run through water that's chest-deep. Friends keep telling me to snap out of it, but that doesn't help. My doctor says I'm in good health and wants to know if you think I should go on anti-depressant drugs?"
**Therapist:** "I recommend anti-depressants only in very severe cases. Here's a pen and the Beck Depression Inventory. It only takes a few minutes and it'll tell us how severe your depression is. I prefer that we retrain your thinking, so you'll learn to stop feeding cognitively distorted ideas into your system."
**Male:** "What kinds of ideas?"
**Therapist:** "Lies. You feel the way you think. There are at least ten common lies, and I want you to learn to recognize all of them. For example, one common lie is that other people's behavior can make you angry. The only thing that makes you angry is your own 'hot thoughts.' Or you may be thinking in all-or-nothing-at-all terms. If a woman turns you down for a date, you tell yourself no woman will ever go out with you."
**Male:** "Isn't that true?"
**Therapist** *(laughing):* "No."

*Films: Midnight Cowboy; Night, Mother; Torchlight; Tokyo Story; Despair; They Shoot Horses, Don't They?*

# DIAGNOSIS

*Identifying or naming symptoms using accepted medical vocabulary.*

The diagnosis of mental problems is a controversial and inexact science.

**Woman:** "A psychiatrist I saw once called me his patient, but you refer to me as a client. Why?"

**Psychologist:** "As a physician, he was trained to use the medical model of illness. I prefer to think of people who consult me as adults with developmental problems, so I call them clients rather than patients. However, a medical-model diagnostic manual—*DSM III-R*—gives labels to all mental problems and aberrations, and therapists must consult it to report to insurance companies on the exact nature of an individual disturbance."

**Woman:** "You have to send a diagnosis to my insurance company?"

**Psychologist:** "Yes. We are all interested in maintaining quality control in treatment. I discuss diagnostic labels with my clients because the bad news is that without my putting a label on you, insurance companies will not pay. And once you're in the insurance company computers, you may be stuck with your label for the rest of your life. Some labels, however, such as 'crisis of adulthood,' have fewer long-range toxic implications than others."

**Student:** "How does someone like me get a mental health checkup to see if I need therapy?"

**Prof:** "There are several ways to get counseling. Start with the campus counseling center. Check the phone book for the county mental health association and a local public clinic, and call for referrals. Or you could inquire of the local hospital, medical association, or therapist referral bureau. You could always look in the pop psychology section of a large bookstore to see if there's a book that describes your condition. If there is, read it and decide if you want to go farther in exploration of what's ailing you."

**Student:** "It's hard to admit I'd like some help or someone to talk to."

*Films: Bedlam, One Flew Over the Cuckoo's Nest, The Snake Pit, Silence of the Lambs, Awakenings.*

# DISPLACEMENT (A DEFENSE)

*Unconsciously redirecting unacceptable feelings that cause anxiety.*

Common example: your boss steps on you, you're angry and upset, then you ruthlessly criticize your secretary.

**Irate wife:** "You'd barely walked through the door when you started yelling at me and the kids. What the hell happened at the office?"
**Frustrated husband:** "A deal I've been working on for months fell through."
**Wife:** "I'm so sorry! You must be really upset, but it's not our fault. Go upstairs and take a long, hot shower. We'll have dinner and then we'll talk."

**Mother:** "Stop trying to pick a fight with your brother. Dad just punished you for using his tools without permission and you're mad at him. I'm not going to let you beat up your brother when you'd really like to take a swing at your dad."
**Punished:** "Why won't he trust me with a crummy wrench?"
**Mother:** "He hasn't forgotten that time you left the tool box out in the rain. Next time ask for his permission and promise you'll put everything away very carefully."

**Father:** "Yesterday I hit my son so hard, it scared me."
**Therapist:** "Did he do something serious?"
**Father:** "Left his rollerblades in the driveway."
**Therapist:** "Then what were you really angry about?"
**Father:** "My wife had just told me she bought another $400 worth of clothes and she's way over her budget."
**Therapist:** "You were really furious with her and you displaced your anger onto your child. Do you have a difficult time showing anger toward your wife?"
**Father:** "My dad wouldn't permit anger to be expressed toward my mother."
**Therapist:** "So you haven't learned how. Better to tell her right on the spot than to hit your kid. What would you like to say to her?"
**Father:** "That she is a stupid, selfish, inconsiderate bitch. That I'm fed up!"
**Therapist:** "That should get her attention."

*Films: Stanley & Livingstone, A Passage to India, The Pawnbroker.*

# DREAMS

*Thoughts, images, and emotions that occur during sleep.*

We are everything we see in our dreams. Each image, person, or event represents some aspect of us. Dreams give us snapshots of our internal condition as we unfold our complex individual nature. We can think of dreams as messages from the acorn that knows our oak tree. They may also symbolically depict relationships among different parts of our body which have no other voice.

**Client:** "How can I tell what a dream means?"
**Therapist:** "Think of it as an announcement of something you need to understand, to think about, or to work through. The symbols in the dream may be archetypal,^ relating to humanity as a whole, but are more probably unique to you, so only you will know what they mean. Sometimes they're puns; the psyche is clever at getting its messages across. When you finally do hit the correct interpretation, you'll feel a zing of recognition."
**Client:** "My dreams do seem to teach me lessons, though often they just process the day's events or show me things to come. But what about recurring dreams?"
**Therapist:** "When you don't get the message, and the acorn determines it's important, the dream recurs or you have a nightmare. The Russians have discovered that dreams even appear to be able to predict disease processes."
**Client:** "What about recording them on my computer?"
**Therapist:** "A journal or computer. Makes no difference. Then they become a unique personal document about your inner life. Periodically read a series of them and two or three unfolding themes will be obvious."
**Client:** "I had a powerful dream three days after my husband died in an auto accident. He came into my bedroom while I was sleeping, stood at the foot of the bed, and said, 'They do a wonderful repair job here,' then turned on his heels and walked back out the door."
**Therapist:** "A Freudian might say that is an example of wish fulfillment. Elisabeth Kubler-Ross and others might see it as an example of the continuity of consciousness after death."
**Client:** "Whatever. I was stunned by it!"

*Films: Tales of Hoffman, The Last Wave, Flatliners, The Black Robe, The Purple Rose of Cairo, All That Jazz, Stardust Memories, Secret Life of Walter Mitty, Dreams.*

# DYSFUNCTIONAL

*Dysfunctional means it doesn't work.*

Children from dysfunctional families may lag behind in physical development or be emotionally handicapped, from mildly disturbed to psychologically crippled. Dysfunctional personal defenses guarantee unhappiness.

**Prof:** "Let's identify some reasons for dysfunction."
**Student:** "We can start before the child is born. During pregnancy, poor nutrition as well as alcohol, nicotine, and other drugs lower birth weight. So the baby is born one-down. After being born, the infant can still be adversely affected by poor nutrition if the mother doesn't know how to feed children properly."
**Another student:** "Where one or both parents are alcoholics or drug abusers, the family is certain to be dysfunctional. Children growing up in chaotic or violent homes will be emotionally disturbed. They don't do as well in school as their more stable peers, and their failures set them up for a lifetime of struggling."
**Prof:** "A few dysfunctional families are cradles of immanence. Some children from chaotic families grow up with great strengths. They survive and our society benefits from their presence. They become powerful change-agents when they channel their pain into creative behavior, community projects, and national politics instead of wallowing around for years in self-pity and victim consciousness.^ Dysfunctional personal defenses like depression in response to life's stresses are useless, because there are many other, more effective ways to react."
**Student:** "Please give an example."
**Prof:** "If you experience loss, you can learn how to mourn, then heal and get on with your life. And you can learn to stop feeding depression-producing thoughts into your system."

**Dysfunctional:** "My family is a mess!"
**Fellow sufferer:** "Whose isn't?"

***Films:*** *True Believer, Rosemary's Baby, The Prince of Tides, Terms of Endearment, Ordinary People, A Long Day's Journey into Night, Avalon.*

# ENVY and JEALOUSY

*Jealousy is an announcement that one feels inferior. Envy is a darker, more destructive form of jealousy which poisons and hardens the heart.*

Envious Cain slew Abel. So we see where envy, translated into action, can lead.

**Jealous:** "Mother always liked you best."

**Wife:** "I saw you looking at that blonde at the party."
**Husband:** "Honey, why are you so jealous? I looked at everyone at one time or another. It didn't mean anything."

**Mother to neighbor:** "I caught Billie pinching the baby this morning. What can I do?"

**Jealous sibling:** "My brother chose first and got the biggest piece of cake!"
**Mother:** "But you cut it. Next time be more careful."

**Weak psychologist:** "I'm jealous of what psychiatrists get paid."
**Weak social worker:** "I'm jealous of what psychologists get paid."

**Married and unhappy:** "I envy my husband's first wife."
**Therapist:** "Why?"
**Unhappy:** "She had him first and they have children together."
**Therapist:** "But he fell out of love with her, divorced her, fell in love with you, married you, and he now sleeps in your bed. You can spoil this marriage with envy."

**Client:** "I envy people who are happy."
**Therapist:** "These feelings are so hostile. You're poisoning yourself."

**Feminist:** "Men have more power than women."
**Therapist:** "What kind of power? Women have the power to create new life in their wombs, which is the most important power on the planet."
**Feminist:** "I mean I want equal pay for equal work."
**Therapist:** "Now you're making sense."

*Films: All About Eve, El, Prix de Beaute (Beauty Prize), Children of Paradise, Star 80, Stage Door.*

# FAMILY

*Father, mother, and child.*

The fundamental triangle of the universe.

**Traditional father:** "I wear the pants in this family! You'll all do as I say, or I'll take a belt to you."
**Mother:** "Yes, we'll do what your father says."
**Kids:** "Don't we have anything to say about anything?"

**Nontraditional father:** "Family council time. I want you home by 10 p.m."
**Kids:** "How about 10:30?"
**Father:** "Okay, this one time. But let me outline what will happen if you fail to make your curfew...."

**Desperate mother:** "You're out of work. I hate to ask you to leave, but I can't get welfare if there's a man here."
**Sad father:** "I'm going to miss you and the children. I'll go and stay with my folks."

**Family therapist:** "I rarely see an intact family these days. It's mostly mothers raising children alone."
**Colleague:** "I see the same thing. And it's not surprising, since more than half of American marriages end in divorce. Do you feel our society is doomed? Or are we going through a major transformation and don't know what the outcome will be?"

**Wounded:** "My father touched my breast once."
**Therapist:** "Did you tell your mother?"
**Wounded:** "No. We couldn't talk to her about anything involving sex."
**Therapist:** "And you never forgot that one touch?"
**Wounded:** "No. I was always tense after that, wondering if he'd do it again."
**Therapist:** "Were you afraid he would or afraid he wouldn't?"

*Films: The Drifting Weeds, Da, The Godfather, Father of the Bride, Hannah and Her Sisters, The Human Comedy, Our Town, Man of Aran, The Best Years of Our Lives, Streetwise, The Empire Strikes Back, The Great Santini, Nanook of the North, Memories of Me, Stranger than Paradise.*

# FANTASY

*A mental product of the imagination, often totally divorced from reality and sometimes depicting reality in exotic, romantic, or delusional forms. Also, daydreams and certain art forms representing situations and ideas that do not exist in the world of direct experience.*

Fantasy can lead to invention, creativity, and more effective expression; it can also mark a deterioration of personality. A therapist must observe the overall functioning of an individual to assess the psychological significance of fantasy.

**Prof:** "Recent research has shown that we all spend a lot of our time daydreaming. We're not even aware of how often we do so."
**Student:** "For me, daydreaming is a form of rehearsal or reality testing, like imagining I just got my grades and they're all A's."
**Prof:** "How can you make the dream come true?"
**Student:** "Study like hell."

**Man:** "I look at the centerfold when I masturbate, and dream she's mine."

**Corporate trainer:** "If you don't see your target clearly, you'll never hit it. What are you aiming for?"
**Frustrated manager:** "Beats me."
**Trainer:** "Exactly!"

**Doctor:** "In diseases like cancer, visualization provides a feeling of empowerment, helps patients take an active role in the healing process, and may even have direct and beneficial physical effects. That's why I recommended that you do imagery exercises in addition to your chemotherapy."
**Cancer patient:** "I am. Three times a day, for twenty minutes at a time, I visualize my white blood corpuscles as armored warriors mobilizing to attack the cancer cells. They love their work; they're ferocious. They devour the cancer, then flush it out of my body."
**Doctor:** "Good riddance!"

*Films: Orphée, Wings of Desire, Zelig, The Illustrated Man, The Serpent and the Rainbow, La Belle et La Bete (Beauty and the Beast)* Cocteau version, *Zardoz, My Private Idaho, Rumble Fish, Roshomon, The Red Balloon, The Man Who Fell to Earth, Star Wars, A Midsummer Night's Dream, Alice in Wonderland, Who Framed Roger Rabbit?*

# FEAR

*A fundamental, instinctual emotion. When we are confronted by a frightening situation, intense, sometimes violent responses take place in the body as we prepare to fight, flee, or conceal our reaction.*

**Students:** "Why are human beings afraid?"
**Prof:** "Fear is one way we protect ourselves, though it can also be misunderstood. Babies are born with an instinctual fear of falling and of loud noises. Physically, at the cellular level, we are born afraid of 'the different.' Ferocious 'warrior' cells and scouts in our bloodstream are on a perpetual seek-and-destroy mission. Let any foreign bacteria or viruses enter the body and millions of killers race to devour them and flush their remains out of the body. The entire immune system is designed to defend the body."
**Student:** "Could this translate into our fear of anyone who's different from us?"
**Prof:** "I think so. There's a fascinating theory that, as infants, when our mothers hold us to the breast and we look into their eyes, we internalize the normal eye-blink rate. Later, if we come upon someone whose blink rate is significantly different—for example, a retarded child whose rate is slower—we recognize it and are repelled. This repulsion and suspicion manifest when people react fearfully to those from different towns, different parts of the country, or with different skin color, eye shape, language."

Some fears are unconscious. Many women, for example, are unconsciously afraid of their fetuses. A growing fetus is, from one point of view, a little parasite, gathering to itself all the mother's resources to build its body. Let the pregnant woman fail to ingest enough calcium and the fetus will take it right out of her teeth.

**Client:** "I am afraid to die."
**Therapist:** "Being alive is wonderful and the idea of giving it up is a source of suffering. That's the suchness of life."
**Client:** "But if we're all going to die, how can we be happy?"
**Therapist:** "That's just the point. We can be happy and grateful that we're alive, not dead yet!"

*Films: King Kong; Sorry, Wrong Number (original version); Cape Fear; Sleeper; Angel Heart; Anguish; Rollercoaster; Savage Attraction; Strangers on a Train; Targets; The Third Man; North by Northwest; Wait until Dark; Ali–Fear Eats the Soul.*

# FEELINGS

*The way we perceive ourselves. We are our feelings. Reactions to the world around us. The way we know we are alive. Feelings may be mental, physical, or both.*

**Man:** "I'm out of touch with my feelings. My wife took the kids and went home to her mother. All I feel is numbness...."
**Minister:** "You're probably in too much pain to feel anything else."

**Woman:** "My mother died and I miss her terribly. I'm so overwhelmed by sorrow, I can't stop crying."
**Counselor:** "When you're grieving, that's normal."

**Client:** "I'm confused. I was deeply in love and I don't understand why I gave up the man."
**Therapist:** "Confusion masks powerful emotions. What's underneath the confusion?"
**Client:** "Pain. He hurt me. When I've been hurt, I often can't speak about it at the moment. I withdraw instead."
**Therapist:** "Why do you withdraw?"
**Client:** "My mother hurt me so badly and so many times, I began to stubbornly refuse to let her see the hurt. I became a rebel and a liar. I lied to her about how terrible I felt and put up a front of cheery invulnerability. So I learned not to disclose pain."
**Therapist:** "That's insightful. Let's talk about how to change this behavior."

**Husband to wife:** "I love you because we have a great sex life, but I hate you at the same time."
**Wife:** "Why?"
**Husband:** "Because you're not meeting all my other needs. I want to be totally taken care of."
**Wife:** "Here I thought I married a grown-up."

**Indignant wife:** "You're insensitive. You never share your feelings and show me tenderness!"
**Husband:** "Why don't we get drunk and screw?"

*Films:* The Deer Hunter, Raging Bull, Dracula (1931 version), *The Twelve Chairs, Stand and Deliver, Seance on a Wet Afternoon, Saboteur, Throne of Blood, Taxi Blues, Hannah and Her Sisters, High Anxiety.*

# FEMINISM

*Concern for the welfare and choices of individual women and also of women in all cultures and societies. Global sisterhood.*

Feminism arose out of women's insistence on the right to vote, their entry into the workplace, their struggles to receive equal pay for equal work, and their wish to change men's minds about the importance of a person's "inner life."

**Wife:** "I went to a meeting of feminists today...."
**Clueless husband:** "Does that mean you're not going to sleep with me anymore?"

**Male boss:** "Down with women's lip. What now?"
**Woman office manager:** "The salary scale in this company is chauvinistic. I want to go on the road, because the salesmen make twice the money I do."
**Boss:** "You're doing too good a job running the operation. Anyway, I've never let women sell, and I'm not going to start now."
**Woman:** "I know the products, the territories, the customers. I can sell as well as any of these guys and if you give me a chance, I'll prove it!"

**Wife:** "Our kids are growing up healthy, but nowadays there's so little appreciation of the vital job of being a wife and mother."
**Husband:** "I appreciate you. I may earn the money, but you make all our lives worth living."
**Wife:** "Thank you for that acknowledgement. I feel a lot of social pressure to get a job."
**Husband:** "Not from me you don't. I respect what you do and I know it's hard work."
**Wife:** "Maybe I've been taking feminism the wrong way."

**Woman assistant prof** *(to Department Head)***:** "The average man takes nine years from Ph.D. to full professor, but the average woman takes 14 years to cover the same ground."
**Male department chairman:** "So?"

*Films: The Bostonians, 9 to 5, Yentl, A Doll's House, City of Women, Daddy's Gone A-Hunting, To Find a Man, Calamity Jane.*

# FORGIVENESS

*The gracious and loving act of letting someone off the hook who has injured you.*

My interpretation of what Jesus meant when he said "turn the other cheek" is that vulnerability and forgiveness lead a person on a spiritually superior path. The Old Testament's demand–"An eye for an eye and a tooth for a tooth"–still leaves you blind and toothless. The most magnanimous moments in your entire life are the moments of forgiveness.

**Therapist:** "Mature people are willing to forgive the stupidity, insensitivity, and violence of others against them in order to get on with their lives."
**Client:** "This doesn't mean they're saying it was okay that they were hurt, does it?"
**Therapist:** "Absolutely not! It means they're willing to heal, they want to heal, because they will feel better, less bitter, when they do. Wise elders have told us to 'forgive and forget.' "

**Wife** *(calm)***:** "Why did you do it?"
**Cheating husband:** "I was mad at you because you made the children more important than me. I love you and I'm terribly sorry I hurt you. Can you forgive me?"
**Wife:** "Yes. I understand now what hurt you. Let's go to bed and talk about it there. Oh, by the way, did you practice safe sex?"

**Husband:** "I've stopped blaming my parents for being alcoholics and fucking up their children's lives, especially mine. So what if we all grew up scared? I'm okay!"
**Wife:** "Honey, I'm so proud of you!"

**Dead Hitler:** "In order for you Jews to get a new kind of freedom from pain, you have to forgive me."
**Jew:** "I agree. Staying angry keeps me stuck. The Jews cannot be annihilated. I cannot be annihilated. Therefore, because I want freedom from hatred, I let go of my rage."
**Hitler:** "Thank God."

*Films: Rapture, Ordinary People, The Informer, The Mission, Christopher Columbus, Les Miserables.*

# FREUD, SIGMUND

*A Viennese physician who practiced in the early 1900s and invented psychoanalysis.^ He coined much of the language of psychology.^*

Because Freud specialized in nervous diseases, many patients told him about their private lives, revealing conflicts, fears, desires, and experiences of sexual abuse. His profound insight came when he recognized that a particular patient whose physical paralysis had no apparent organic cause seemed to be expressing, through her body, an unconscious emotional conflict. He not only realized that every person has an Unconscious^ but also that "dreams are the royal road to the Unconscious."

**Psychology prof:** "Freud's ideas on childhood sexuality and personality development are as astute and controversial today as they were when he first startled the medical community with them between 1894 and 1900."

**Student:** "Okay, but what's a Freudian slip?"

**Prof:** "Another way to access the Unconscious. When a word or phrase we didn't intend to say slips out of our mouths, or we mis-hear, or have an odd misunderstanding, we realize it is not a mistake but a clue to something stirring underneath, in the Unconscious."

**Student:** "I'll have to pay more attention to myself when I say something that requires correction. But...what else about him?"

**Prof:** "Freud theorized that human personality is a kind of energy system, motivated by two different, powerful drives—one toward death, one toward life. He believed aggressiveness and violence are expressions of the death drive, and that erotic pleasure-seeking expresses the life drive, which he considered to be the more important. He saw sexual symbols in everyday objects, though he did say, 'Sometimes a cigar is just a cigar.' "

**Student:** "Is there anything else I should know for the midterm?"

**Prof:** "By 1923, he developed a model of the mind with three structural parts: id, ego, and superego.^ Jung^ and other colleagues disagreed with Freud and they all went their separate ways. Nevertheless, he was one of the greatest thinkers of our century. And if it wasn't for Freud, I wouldn't have a job."

*Films: Freud, The Secret Diary of Sigmund Freud.*

# GOD

*The awesome Creator. A supernatural, superhuman Being or Force with many names worldwide. The Higher Power of Alcoholics Anonymous.*

"The living spirit is eternally renewed and pursues its goal in manifold and inconceivable ways throughout the history of mankind." –C.G. Jung

**God-loving woman:** "I don't know how to describe the grandeur and awesomeness of the light in my concept of God. By comparison, the endless, boundless universe is smaller."
**God-loving man:** "I feel the same way."

In a group therapy session for compulsive overeaters:
**Fat client** (*standing on a table in the middle of the room*): "I am mad at God! My life is shit!"
**Therapist:** "It's God's fault?"
**Fat:** "Yes. It's all His fault."
**Therapist:** "Are you sure we're not talking about your father? Most people's feelings about God come from their experiences with their dads."
**Fat:** "You mean I'm blaming God for what my father did to me?"
**Rest of the group:** "And you're eating over it!"

**Wealthy man:** "Making money is the most important thing I have to do in this life."
**Friend:** "Is money your god? Money is just coming along so you can get what you want. What do you want to do with your money?"

**Woman client:** "I worship my father."
**Therapist:** "No wonder you can't find a man. What ordinary man could compete with a god?"

**Feminist:** "I'm sure God is a woman!"

*Films: Inherit the Wind; The Robe; The Last Temptation of Christ; The Mahabharata; Hallelujah; The Passion of Joan of Arc; Godspell; Jesus Christ, Superstar; Jesus of Nazareth; Ordet; Sister Act; Say Amen, Somebody; The Greatest Story Ever Told; Samson and Delilah.*

# GRACE

*Christian: unmerited divine assistance.*
*Transpersonal: the true condition of existence, though not usually recognized until we attain sufficient personal and spiritual maturity.*

That one sperm out of multiple millions from one's father and one egg out of a quarter-million from one's mother ever got together so we could have a life is amazing. The fact that we survived infancy and childhood, and are still alive, is why I say all of us are living in a state of grace from the moment we are born.

**Child:** "Daddy, that song we sang in church today ... 'Amazing Grace'? What does it mean?"
**Father:** "It means we are all blessed every minute of every day. And I believe the generosity of that blessing is wonderful for you to know about. The energy from the sun warms our whole planet and makes life possible here, but it's only one trillionth of the energy the sun puts out every day. And if the earth were cooling one degree more slowly per century, we wouldn't even be here! Life simply wouldn't be possible!"
**Child:** "Did God plan all of that so perfectly?"
**Father:** "I believe it. That's what amazing grace is about."

**Surfer:** "When I was surfing on the coast of Africa, even the baboons became silent to watch the sun rise. I feel a momentous kind of grace at that time of the day, which is why I like to be out in the water early in the morning. When I sit on my board and watch the day break, I feel glad to be alive."
**Buddy:** "I know exactly what you mean, but there are few people I could even discuss this with. My folks wouldn't understand it."
**Surfer:** "Too bad, huh?"

**Pilot:** "Sometimes when I'm flying, I look down on the earth and see all those little lights and I'm filled with love for humanity...for each and every person below. I feel like blessing them all with my love. Am I crazy?"
**Wife:** "No. And I don't ever remember being so touched by something you've said as I am right this minute."

*Films: Resurrection, Close Encounters of the Third Kind, The Medicine Man.*

# GRIEF (NOT DEPRESSION)

*Grief is the normal, painful experience of mourning that follows a severe loss.*

Grief is natural after the death of a relative or close friend (personal grief) or of beloved leaders, like J.F.K. or Martin Luther King, Jr. (collective grief). Grief of either kind is cumulative unless it is experienced through mourning. Mourning may last one to three years, depending on the severity of the loss. It comes and goes in waves and cannot be short-circuited. If grief is not released, it can spill out when least expected.

**Widow** *(crying)*: "My husband died three months ago, and the family just goes on as if nothing had happened."

**Therapist:** "I'm sorry. In the old days, when death came, mourners howled, tore their clothes, poured ashes over themselves, and sat on boxes for a week while people brought them casseroles and chicken soup. For a year, they wore black clothes or black armbands or black ribbons pinned on their lapels. Everyone in the community could see these visible signs of mourning and provide support and comfort. Recently, we Americans have been so busy denying death that most of us can't even talk about it."

**Widow:** "At the funeral home, the corpse was decorated with so much make-up I hardly recognized the body. It was as if we were in a fantasy, pretending the body was not already decomposing, ignoring the fact that no one lives there anymore. It hurt."

**Therapist:** "Some Americans are actually freezing dead bodies in the hope of resurrecting them someday. Never mind. How long were you married?"

**Widow:** "Fifteen years."

**Therapist:** "After fifteen years of loving him, the pain of his death won't go away in three months. Have you been crying?"

**Widow:** "Every day."

**Therapist:** "Well, just keep it up and don't make any important decisions for a year. The pain will ease and then return, ease and return. When Grandma said 'Good grief!' she knew what she was talking about."

*Films: The Rose Tattoo; Dead Calm; JFK; Ordinary People; The Stone Boy; Truly, Madly, Deeply.*

# GUILT

*A learned sense of wrongdoing (as compared with fear, an instinctual emotion); a consequence of real or imagined acts or thoughts that are unacceptable to oneself because they go against either one's own standards or conventional moral and social standards.*

Healthy guilt: An appropriate response when we've done something terrible.

Unhealthy, poisoning guilt: The way we pay to keep on doing what we know is wrong or damaging to us...and pay, and pay, and pay. (Parents, government, schools, advertisers, and the Church use guilt to control behavior.)

**Client:** "When I cheat on my wife I feel guilty."
**Therapist:** "You're suffering?"
**Client:** "Yes. Take the pain away."
**Therapist:** "That's some fantasy you have going!"

**Client:** "When I beat one of my children I feel guilty."
**Therapist:** "Why not stop doing both?"

**Client:** "I never pay what I really owe in income tax. I feel guilty and the IRS may get me!"
**Therapist:** "But feeling guilty doesn't change your behavior. Let's drop the guilt and talk about what part of you wants to get away with anything it can."

**German Catholic Theologian:** "I feel guilty that the Church did little to stop the Nazis' wartime slaughter, both in the concentration camps and by bombing, of thirteen million people."
**Questioner:** "How are you using your guilt?"
**Theologian:** "I am working tirelessly for Church reform."

**Teenager** *(yawning)*: "This book is incredibly boring."
**Guilt-making teacher:** "That may be true, but a lot of the community's tax money was spent to buy it, so show a little appreciation."

**Guilt-making mother:** "I don't care if you don't like the taste of it. Other children are starving, so eat it."
**Kid:** "Throw up on this yuck!"

*Films: Macbeth, The Woman Next Door, Defending Your Life, The Tell-Tale Heart, Hamlet.*

# HALLUCINATIONS

*Things heard, touched, seen, or otherwise felt in the body, and experienced as if there were actual physical stimulation, though there is none.*

Hallucinations are a symptom of severe mental disturbance.

**Psychiatrist** *(doing in-take exam at mental hospital)*: "Tell me about what's going on in your body."
**Patient:** "My head is on fire all the time. The only relief I ever get is when cool water drips down all around my head, like now. I feel it running down my face."
**Psychiatrist:** "We'll put you on medication to see how quickly we can put out the fire."
**Patient:** "My regular doctor is a fireman, too."

**Prof:** "Give me some examples of psychotic hallucinations."
**Student:** "A patient says, 'Snakes are crawling around in my belly' or 'A snake has crawled into my vagina and lives there.' "
**Prof:** "Yes, those are good. In one case I know of, a woman was certain someone was stretching her skin away from her body. She felt her hands and legs becoming enormous and the skin on her head being pulled out as far as two feet. She suffered terribly."
**Student:** "But what's the difference between hallucinations and the states of consciousness just before waking or falling asleep when we sometimes see unusual and puzzling images?"
**Prof:** "Those transitional states of consciousness^ are normal and are called 'hypnogogic,' to acknowledge the fact that the person is not in his or her ordinary sleeping or waking consciousness.^ Some people call these experiences waking dreams."

**Young experimenter:** "One of the most foolish and dangerous things I've done in my life happened at a concert. Someone passed around acid tabs, so I dropped one. I had bad flashbacks that lasted over a year."
**Friend:** "What happened?"
**Young:** "My head filled with light and energy and my mind was full of anxiety. My hands started to shake. If I was driving, I had to pull off the road because I couldn't think, let alone drive. It was terrifying."
**Friend:** "You're lucky you didn't do any permanent brain damage."

*Films: The Ruling Class, The Stunt Man, F/X, The Fisher King, The Treasure of the Sierra Madre, Greed, Delusion, Brazil, Hour of the Wolf. For other films related to this topic, see list on page 88.*

# HEALING

*Repair of body, mind, and/or spirit.*

When we have a minor cut, blood instantly fills the wound and it scabs over; beneath the scab, armies of cells are busy with repairs. No conscious commands from us are needed. However, healing more serious physical illness and wounds to the mind and spirit requires our conscious involvement.

**Limping junkie** *(at Crisis Center)*: "I came in to see somebody today because I was scared. I fell down the stairs while I was loaded and broke my ankle. I need help."
**Social Worker:** "The speed of the healing depends on the severity of the break, your general health, the food you eat, your psychological condition. If you're depressed, physical healing slows down."
**Junkie:** "I want to work on psychological wounds."
**Social:** "Oh? What wounds are we talking about?"
**Junkie:** "My mind is fucked up and I feel rotten about myself."
**Social:** "This'll be hard work, because attitudes toward the self are formed at a very young age. A negative self-concept^ may take years to change, and in some cases can't be changed at all."
**Junkie:** "Can you explain my addiction to heroin?"
**Social:** "Studies of men who become addicted to heroin reveal that when they were between four and seven years old, their mothers disappeared. The mothers died, abandoned the family, or were hospitalized for long periods."
**Junkie:** "My little sister died when I was six."
**Social:** "Then your mother went into deep mourning, perhaps for a whole year. She was emotionally unavailable to you. You experienced that withdrawal as being abandoned by her."
**Junkie:** "You mean I was set up for addiction?"
**Social:** "Yes. It's a pattern. You wrote an unconscious lifescript that says: 'It's my fault that my mother isn't here for me. Whatever is wrong with me can't be fixed. I feel depressed and unloveable. No one else will love me, either. I'll do anything not to feel this bad, including shoving a needle in my arm.' "
**Junkie:** "It'll take a miracle to get me out of this hole I'm in."
**Social:** "Let's work to create one. I'll put you in detox today."

*Films: The Doctor, The Hospital, Awakenings, The Snake Pit, Man with the Golden Arm, Resurrection, City of Joy, Dances with Wolves.*

# HOSTILITY SYNDROME

*A collection of symptoms, behaviors, and attitudes that are common responses to new ideas.*

**Prof:** "The Hostility Syndrome is how some people react to new ideas. According to research, two-thirds of the adult population become anxious because new ideas disturb their inner sense of balance."
**Students:** "How anxious?"
**Prof:** "From mild discomfort to anxiety to progressively more and more hostility until they want to send the creative person to his death and burn his books, paintings, and whatever he's created."
**Students:** "Give us an example."
**Prof:** "The philosopher Socrates was killed because he was teaching the youth of Athens ideas that were threatening to local politics."
**Students:** "Any others?"
**Prof:** "Jesus was sent up to Calvary for new ideas that were threatening to the Establishment."
**Students:** "Who else?"
**Prof:** "When the French Impressionist painters first exhibited their work, people were outraged because the paintings were so different from what the public was used to seeing."
**Students:** "And today?"
**Prof:** "Salman Rushdie was marked for death for writing *The Satanic Verses*. His ideas are revolting to Muslim fundamentalist religious leaders."
**Students:** "And what about the other one-third of the population, who don't become anxious when they hear a new idea? What are they doing?"
**Prof:** "They're open-minded. They test, they examine, they try out new things. If they don't like them, they discard what doesn't work. If they are enthusiastic, they honor the creator with prizes, recognition, and fame."
**Students:** "Okay, we understand. What is your point?"
**Prof:** "My question to you is, 'Are you going to be part of the problem or part of the solution?' "

*Films: Fiddler on the Roof; Tucker: The Man and His Dream; Inherit the Wind; Hawaii; Babette's Feast; Thelma & Louise; Driving Miss Daisy.*

# HYPNOSIS

*A technique to alter one's state of consciousness for the purpose of bringing about changes in sensations, perceptions, and thought patterns. In a hypnotic state, one becomes highly suggestible.*

Despite much scoffing by psychologists, researchers have been able to verify the existence of "trance logic." They did so through a series of experiments in which hypnotized subjects freely mixed hallucinations suggested by the hypnotist with other perceptions based on real logic and events. Another kind of trance, well-known among those who drive long, boring miles on the highway, is "road hypnosis." Many drivers find themselves in their car, at their destination, but unable to remember how they got there, though some part of them was, in fact, driving.

**Hypnotist** (*working on smoking cessation*): "Using focused concentration, I'll lead you into a trance."
**Subject:** "If I am willing to cooperate with you, what will happen?"
**Hypnotist:** "I'll make post-hypnotic suggestions and you'll act on them after awakening. This is much the same as what Freud did in his study and treatment of hysteria, but that proved impractical since not everyone can be hypnotized and the effects are frequently only temporary. We'll see what happens in your case."
**Subject:** "I'll try anything! I'm so hooked on nicotine! Why I ever started smoking, I'll never know!"
**Hypnotist:** " 'Why' is not important. We want behavioral change."

**Midwife:** "In 1958, the American Medical Association approved the use of hypnosis in medicine to relieve pain in childbirth or dentistry, especially when anesthetics are dangerous or impractical. Do you want hypnosis during labor?"
**Pregnant:** "Does it work?"
**Midwife:** "Yes, although most obstetricians use conventional anesthetics."

**Man-on-the-make:** "Look deep into my eyes...."

*Films: Freud, Svengali, Black Magic, Fear in the Night, Abbott and Costello Meet Frankenstein, Road to Rio, On a Clear Day You Can See Forever, The Court Jester, Divorce American Style, The Search for Bridey Murphy.*

# ID, EGO, SUPEREGO

*Terms coined by Freud to represent what he regarded as the three major aspects of human consciousness. The Id is our primordial, instinctual, animal nature that demands immediate gratification. Ego is the ordinary, everyday mind in which we live, usually reasonable but often very inflated. Superego is the conscience, driver, corrector, punisher; it represents the moral standards of society as taught by parents.*

Jung and Freud disagreed about these layers of consciousness. Jung thought the personality is best described as: *persona* ^ (the ideal we try to show to the world), *ego*^ (in which we actually live), and *shadow*^ (the dark side we don't know about and usually don't want to know about).

**Voice of the Id:**
"I want what I want when I want it."
"I need two thousand pairs of shoes."–Imelda Marcos
"I'll have the dessert first. As a matter of fact, I won't have anything else after the dessert."
See: Scarlett O'Hara in *Gone With the Wind.*

**Voice of the Ego:**
"Who cares if I'm two hours late for my concert. My fans would wait two days to hear me play."
"It may sound self-righteous, but it's hard for me to apologize for my rare mistakes."
See: Michael Douglas' role in *Wall Street.*

**Voice of the Superego:**
"You're not good enough!" ...spoken to yourself in rejection, after which your inner voices take up the cries:
"You're not working hard enough!"
"You're not wanted!"
"You ought to be ashamed of yourself!"
"You'll rot in hell!"
See: Father in *The Heiress.*

**Therapist:** "Why are you here?"
**Client:** "Nobody takes me seriously."
**Therapist:** "You've got to be kidding."

*Films: Mutiny on the Bounty, Moby Dick, The Competition, Little Big Man.*

# INCEST

*Sexual intercourse between children and either older family members, close relatives, or close friends of the family.*

Sadism^ and lack of remorse characterize most adults who violate children. Whether or not the children are willing partners is not the issue, even though we know some children can be very seductive. Our focus here is on the adults.

**Incestuous, lustful father** *(to daughters)*: "You belong to me and it's my right to initiate you."

**Prostitute:** "Do you have a 'whore theory,' about why I might have let myself be turned out by my pimp?"
**Therapist:** "Were you involved in incest? Early incest leads to serious emotional problems for girls. They often become promiscuous adolescents, then prostitutes, or anorexics, or alcoholics, and some have to be hospitalized for severe compulsive overeating."

**Frightened woman:** "My father talked me into intercourse when I was eight. When I was fifteen, my mother committed suicide in a fit of rage after she discovered us in bed."
**Therapist:** "What a story! Intercourse with your father gave you sexual pleasure, didn't it? At the same time you felt guilty about taboo sex...a killing load of conflict, shame, and guilt for a young girl to bear."
**Frightened:** "I'm not happy. I live with a married man. He's black. I'm white. And I'm getting fatter every day. Look at me. I weigh 190 pounds."
**Therapist:** "You're repeating your pattern...living in conflict, and doing so with a married, unavailable man, in a taboo relationship. The only thing you know how to do is stuff down all this intolerable pain and conflict with food. But there are other alternatives. Let's discuss them."

In an "unusual" gesture of comfort, a mother has intercourse with her son in *Murmur of the Heart*, then things appear to go on as normal in the family.

*Films: Scarface; Toys in the Attic; A View from the Bridge; Chinatown; Country Dance; La Luna; My Lover, My Son; Nuts; Murmur of the Heart.*

# INTELLIGENCE

*Mental and physical abilities that, although inherited, can be enhanced by education and life-experience. Not the same as creativity.*

Any given intelligence-test score–for instance, an I.Q. ("Intelligence Quotient")–is only one possible result of a specific test on a particular day. It represents a *partial* (and variable) assessment of a whole person.

Different kinds of intelligence include:

*Common sense.* The kinds of things we learn while walking in the woods beside a flowing stream, or in a meadow. Also: plain, everyday street smarts.

*Linguistic.* The ability to read, write, pun, understand the lingo, teach, and give speeches.

*Logical-mathematical.* The ability to reason, use math the way computer wizards, scientists, navigators, engineers, and accountants do.

*Spatial.* The ability to mentally rotate shapes in space and accurately imagine the outcome. The skills of artists, designers, architects, builders, and mechanics.

*Musical.* Perfect pitch, singing on key, playing instruments, composing, and musical memory.

*Bodily-kinesthetic.* Body mastery. Athletic and dance abilities that we see in jugglers, gymnasts, and professional sports figures.

*Social.* The ability to read faces and body postures, to pour oil on troubled waters, to sell anything, to mediate conflicts.

*Originality.* The ability to create something astonishing.

*Wisdom.* The ability to discern patterns in life-experience.

**Woman counselor:** "You're 24 years old and can't get a girlfriend? Being successful with women takes basic social intelligence. Let's start with reading faces. I'll make faces, you tell me what they mean. What is your interpretation of this facial expression?"
**Interpersonal illiterate:** "You want to make love."
**Counselor:** "No way! This look says, 'You're repulsive.' "

**Frustrated wife:** "How can you be so smart about some things and so stupid about others?"
**Husband:** "It's easy."

*Films: How Green Was My Valley, The Lawnmower Man, Tim.*

# INNER CHILD

*A child part of ourselves that lives in the Unconscious.^ If our child has been psychologically wounded, then healing that child is part of our adult developmental work. We may have several inner children, all of whom can have different identities.*

A controversy is raging about whether or not inner children can ever be healed. What's indisputable, though, is that these inner children are powerful, directly involved in adult disease processes, and can take over and direct our interactions with others with no warning and completely out of our awareness. When an adult says, "It's scary," you are hearing the voice of a child who is dominant for that moment.

One of the best ways to differentiate among the many inner children is to look at children in films and what they symbolize:
The Wounded Child: *Morgan!, Sybil, Children of Hiroshima.*
The Evil Child: *The Bad Seed, Firestarter.*
The Magical Child: *ET, The Little Prince.*
The Angry Child: *The Tin Drum.*
The Perfect Child: *Little Miss Marker.*
The Creative Child: *Home Alone.*
The Repressed Child: *Little Lord Fauntleroy.*
The Retarded Child: *A Child Is Waiting.*
The Irrepressible Child: *Tom Sawyer.*
The Deprived Child: *Dead End Kids.*
The Nazi Child: *Tomorrow the World.*
The Uncouth but Loveable Child: *Huckleberry Finn.*
The Sexual Child: *Lolita.*
The Senex (old beyond its years) Child: *Paper Moon.*
The Doomed Child: *Pixote.*
The Charming Child: *Little Women.*
The Crippled Child: *Annie's Coming Out.*
The Persecuted Child: *Au Revoir Les Enfants.*
The Innocent Child: *Oliver Twist.*
The Frightened Child: *Europa, Europa.*
The Nervy Child: *Annie.*
The Initiated Child: *The Wizard of Oz.*
The Handicapped Child: *The Miracle Worker* (1962).

# JUNG, CARL GUSTAV

*A Swiss physician who formed a close association with Sigmund Freud after they met in 1906. A prolific, boundary-breaking writer, metaphysician, and mystic.*

Jung split with Freud because of disagreements about the nature and structure of the Unconscious^ and the directions psychoanalytic theory should take, then he founded his own school of psychoanalysis,^ Analytic Psychology. After studying similarities in myths, dreams, and world religions, he developed the idea of the Collective Unconscious,^ a psychic envelope of the instincts, urges, images, and memories of the entire human species that enfolds the world.

**Student:** "Jung had a name for the major forces in the Collective Unconscious,^ didn't he?"

**Prof:** "Yes. He called them Archetypes,^ and felt they could be discerned in the world's myths. Further, because so many of those myths are stories about the conflict between opposites, he concluded that the aim of psychic life is to bring our internal opposites into wholeness. He referred to this process of individuation, of creating a new whole person, as the 'journey of the soul.' "

**Student:** "Didn't he coin the terms 'introvert' and 'extrovert,' too?"

**Prof:** "Yes. Introverts are inward-looking, quiet, shy; extroverts are outward-looking, have high energy, are sociable. Jung theorized that each type must learn balance. The introvert needs to become more aware of practical, everyday existence; the extrovert more aware of his inner world. Life is about balance."

**Student:** "What else was noteworthy about Jung?"

**Prof:** "As a major theorist, he was willing to explore taboo areas, such as spirituality. This was very alarming to some contemporary psychologists, a fact which is reflected, for example, in the 1986 Random House edition of *Psychology Today*, an otherwise excellent 758-page textbook, where he is not mentioned once, despite the fact that his collected manuscripts amount to more than 22 volumes."

**Student:** "Fascinating! I knew some of his views made him the focus of condemnation and scoffing by many secular psychologists."

*Films: Boundaries of the Soul: Explorations in Jungian Analysis; Jung on Film;* "The Wisdom of the Dream" series: *A Life of Dreams, Inheritance of Dreams, A World of Dreams.*

# JUSTIFICATION

*Defending our behavior and ideas by taking any position, no matter how absurd, ridiculous, or disgusting, to make ourselves right.*

"There's a sucker born every minute."–P.T. Barnum

**Husband** (*pouring a drink*): "Hard day at the office."
**Martyrwife:** "But you've already had three martinis!"
**Husband:** "One more should help me really relax."
**Wife:** "Why don't you admit you're an alcoholic!"
**Husband:** "No, I'm not. I'm just tense."

**Disgusted mother:** "You gave your brother a bloody nose over one baseball card?"
**Bully:** "He touched it!"

**Sheriff:** "You boys all raped an unconscious girl!"
**Gang:** "She was drinking. That's asking for it."

**Savings and Loan crook:** "We just made some poor real estate investments. That wasn't stealing."

**Ambitious General:** "The president wasn't doing his job. The army had to take over."

**Police officer:** "But you all heard the woman screaming...."
**Passives:** "We didn't call the police because we didn't want to get involved. Getting involved is messy...."

**Inspector:** "This building is a joke. You have 140 violations, including rats, roaches, and no heat."
**Tenement landlord:** "What's the use of fixing it up when the tenants won't take care of it anyway?"

**Doctor:** "You have AIDS and you're still having unprotected sex with any number of people?"
**Vicious:** "I'm dying."

**Client to therapist:** "Thank you for a year of insight." Pulls a loaded gun. "But now you know too much."

*Films: Other People's Money, Wall Street, Two for the Seesaw, Pacific Heights, JFK, Born on the Fourth of July.*

# LETTING GO

*Releasing the past, the deceased, the traumas, the violations, the guilt, and all treasured wounds.*

Letting go sometimes takes years to accomplish, but it must be done in order to be fully present in this *now* moment of your life.

**Widow:** "It's two years and I'm still crying. I haven't forgiven him for dying and leaving me."
**Therapist:** "Have you removed all his personal belongings from your house and recycled his old clothes or are you still maintaining a shrine to his memory?"
**Widow:** "I can't just throw his things away."
**Therapist:** "So you really haven't completed your mourning. I wonder why. Do you have some guilt about things you did or said in your relationship?"

**Wealthy man:** "I just can't seem to stop worrying."
**Therapist:** "What are you worrying about?"
**Man:** "Losing my money. I have real estate investments, a big pension coming, $700,000 in cash in the bank, my home is paid for, my taxes are low, but I'm so afraid I can't even live my life."
**Therapist:** "This feels like an anxiety disorder to me. Let's work out a treatment plan."

**Reclusive man:** "I can't dance."
**Therapist:** "You mean you don't want to. When someone says the word 'can't' to me, I always substitute 'don't want to.' What will happen if you dance?"
**Man:** "I'll make a fool of myself and people will laugh at me. Dancing, according to my father and mother, is sexual and sinful."
**Therapist:** "Join a gym and begin to exercise with other people. Play passionate music at home and move your body to it. Watch TV programs where kids are dancing. Sign up for an aerobics class or a dance class. They're full of women. Report back next week."
**Man:** "Roger! Over and out!"
**Therapist:** "You needn't salute when you leave."

*Films: The Rose Tattoo, Flashdance, Dirty Dancing, Red River, Sophie's Choice, The Frisco Kid, An American in Paris, Sweet Charity.*

# LOVE

*Personal (conditional) love: affection based on admiration or benevolence. Warm, passionate attachment, enthusiasm, or devotion.*
*Impersonal (unconditional) love: a constant, dispassionate, continuous acceptance.*

Self-love: The basis of self-respect, on which a healthy personality can be created. Self-love gone wrong, carried to self-obsession, is narcissism.^ Other kinds of love: romantic/erotic; familial; brotherly (all humanity); love of country (patriotism); of the whole planet (global consciousness); of money (greed).

**Husband:** "Now that we've been married two years, I'm beginning to know you better. You have all sorts of dimensions I couldn't have even guessed...and you always leave the top off the toothpaste."
**Wife:** "Since the baby was born, my capacity for loving is larger than I ever thought possible."

**WW II vet:** "When the flag comes into view and I hear the band playing a march, I always get a thrill. What I love about democracy is that each person's thoughts are precious, whether I agree with them or not."

**Minister:** "Show your brotherly love by feeding the hungry."
**Congregation member:** "I give the first dime out of every dollar I earn to charities."
**Minister:** "That's very generous. And of course you must also save a dime, then reserve another for pleasure. Then pay your bills."

**Son:** "I'll always love my family, my community, and my country first, but I'm starting to think about myself as a global citizen. I love the whole precious little planet."
**Father:** "I thought all this fuss about ecology was bunk, but I was asleep on my feet."

*Films: Cyrano de Bergerac, Love Story, Sylvia, A Man and a Woman, The Good Earth, Rebecca, Love Among the Ruins, Wuthering Heights, Tristan and Isolde, The Taming of the Shrew, The Cranes Are Flying, Woman in the Dunes, The African Queen, My Favorite Year, Last Tango in Paris.*

# MASOCHISM

*Finding relief or pleasure from either inflicting pain on yourself or from having someone else do it.*

Masochists associate being hurt with relief from guilt or with sexual arousal. As children they were often abused and enraged, but could not direct their anger toward a tormentor, so they turned it on themselves and became self-abusive.^ They are also capable of inflicting pain on others, which is called "sadomasochism."

**Daughter:** "Bob beat me up so I left him."
**Mother:** "Well, your father did it to me. I certainly deserved it when I spent too much money or couldn't keep you kids under control."
**Daughter:** "Mom, that's ridiculous! No one deserves to be beaten. When I married I didn't realize I was picking out someone who would treat me the same rotten way Dad treated you. I don't know how you stuck it out all these years."
**Mother:** "I love him."
**Daughter:** "You must love pain, too. Since I've been in group therapy, I see my pattern is just like yours. My therapist says I have to be very careful or I'll pick out a brutal man again."

**Woman:** "My husband wants me to beat him during sex. I refuse."
**Minister:** "Perhaps he has a load of guilt around sexuality. Was he severely punished as a child?"
**Woman:** "So he says. But this is very difficult for me to handle. I love him and I don't want to hurt him."
**Minister:** "Will he come in for a talk? If he's not willing to work on it, your marriage may end, because he'll go elsewhere for the particular combination of pleasure and pain he's seeking."

**Client:** "I want to hurt myself. I'm always thinking about burning my arms with my cigarettes."
**Therapist:** "I'm glad you came in to see me, because this is serious."

**Wife:** "I feel like killing my husband a lot of the time, but if I make him angry enough to hit me, I don't feel so guilty about my murderous thoughts."

*Films: Blue Velvet, Dangerous Liaisons, Silence of the Lambs, Sleeping with the Enemy, Mine Own Executioner.*

# MEDITATION

*The practice of quieting the body and centering the consciousness through controlled breathing, imagery, and concentration.*

Research shows that meditation lowers blood-pressure, slows down the heart, and leads to deep relaxation. But an even more striking effect is that it opens personal awareness to transpersonal realms, realms that are usually unknown to contemporary persons, and are not ordinarily available to waking consciousness.

**Student:** "There are so many methods of meditation. How does a person decide which to try?"
**Prof:** "By experimenting with instructional audio or video tapes, or by following written directions, or by finding a meditation teacher. General instructions are similar. Start with an empty stomach. Sit quietly, either on the floor or on a chair with a straight back. Be comfortable...not too hot, not too cold. Wear loose clothes. Begin with five minutes, then increase to twenty or longer. But even five minutes of closed eyes and quiet breathing is better than nothing."
**Student:** "I read about Brugh Joy's spiral meditation, which involves placing your hands over the body's energy centers–the chakras–in a spiral pattern. Another technique he developed takes you to a sacred temple by the sea."
**Prof:** "Very powerful. Buddhist Vipassana meditation begins with learning to sit quietly and to follow your own breath in and out of your lungs, observing thoughts that enter your mind, then releasing them. Zen Buddhist meditation is generally done facing a wall, with the eyes partially open. Students use various methods to quiet the mind: counting breaths, following breaths, examining and dismissing any thought that intrudes, until total presence of mind is achieved."
**Student:** "What about using chants or a mantra?"
**Prof:** "A mantra, a phrase repeated over and over again, like 'Lord Jesus Christ have mercy,' will open the well of the Unconscious.^ Chanting has the same effect. It can take you in deep. Staring at a painting that has a centerpoint, or at a candle, can bring you into a meditative state."

**Novice to guru:** "Will it help me grow hair?"

**Films:** *The Razor's Edge* (Bill Murray version)*, Meetings with Remarkable Men.*

# MENOPAUSE

*Gradual cessation of menstruation that occurs as hormone production by the ovaries ends. A potentially empowering passage from the time of childbearing into the time of eldership.*

Post-menopausal women can become wise elders or just plain old. Menopause may last as long as ten years and be a smooth transition, or it can be accompanied by disturbing physical symptoms.

**Thirty-four-year-old daughter** (*to menopausal mother*): "Why are you so sad and blue these days?"
**Menopausal:** "I'm grieving about my womb. I know I'll never have any more babies."
**Daughter:** "You had your last baby 34 years ago and I know you don't really want more babies!"
**Menopausal:** "But the fact that I can't have them is a loss. According to the usual scheme of things, my grandchildren are supposed to be coming along. You've been living with Rick for ten years. Any plans to get married and have children?"
**Daughter:** "No."
**Menopausal:** "I was afraid of that. Soon I'll also be mourning the grandchildren I never had."
**Daughter:** "Wait a minute! You feel hurt because I'm not getting married and you want me to feel it right along with you. Stop trying to put your pain on me."

**Self-loathing woman:** "Well, the curse is finally coming to an end."
**Daughter:** "What curse?"
**Mother:** "You know...menstruation."
**Daughter:** "If it wasn't for the Women's Movement, I might feel the same way about my periods. But since I took a body-image workshop, I really love that time of the month. I have a terrific release of energy that I feel is cleansing and very good for me."
**Mother:** "Maybe I was born too soon...."

**Enthusiastic wife:** "Let's make love!"
**Husband:** "Menopause certainly hasn't turned you off!"
**Wife:** "Were you worried?"
**Husband:** "Frankly, yes."

*Films: The Effect of Gamma Rays on Man-in-the-Moon Marigolds, A Woman of a Certain Age, The Subject Was Roses.*

# MULTIPLE PERSONALITY

*Two or more personalities in the same body. Schizophrenics frequently display a "split personality," with each part unknown to the other.*

Many therapists feel that various seed potentials, struck at birth, are contained in the Unconscious^ of every normal person. These potentials–inner children, inner adolescents, inner young adults and mature adults, and elders–may or may not develop, depending on life circumstances. Each literally speaks with a distinctly different voice, and we may slip from one such personality into another without awareness.

**Husband to wife:** "I don't understand it. You're forty years old but when your father comes around, you act like a little girl."
**Wife:** "That's just how I feel when I'm with him."

**Therapist to client named Betty:** "I want to talk to one of your inner children who's involved with your sex life. We'll do a voice dialogue. Does she have a name?"
**Betty:** "Yes. She's Little Miss Prissy."
**Therapist:** "Bring her out and put her in that chair over there."
(Client moves to another chair in the therapy room.)
**Therapist:** "Now, Miss Prissy, let's talk about sex. What do you think about it?"
**Prissy's voice:** "It's messy, it's violent, it's animal behavior."
**Therapist:** "Is that why you don't let Betty have orgasms?"
**Prissy:** "If I had my way, she wouldn't have sex at all."
**Therapist:** "So you stop her from sexual pleasure?"
**Prissy:** "Yes."
**Therapist:** "Betty move back to your original chair. Do you see how this inner child is involved with your sex life?"
**Betty:** "Yes. Kids don't have sex, and when I'm ready to go to bed with my husband, the child takes over."

**Woman:** "I'm a professionally trained manager, but with my boss, sometimes I'm so embarrassed I can't talk."
**Therapist:** "When that happens, you'll know one of your inner children has taken over."

*Films: The Three Faces of Eve, Sybil, Lizzie, Dr. Jekyll and Mr. Hyde, Prelude to a Kiss, The Boston Strangler.*

# MYSTICISM

*That which deals with the transcendent "mysteries" all around us. Personal and direct knowing of Spirit, God, the Life Force, Jesus, Buddha, the Tao, Shiva, Vishnu, Quan-Yin, Mary, or the Divine aspects of Life by whatever name they may be known. Encounters with forces which inspire us to noble thoughts and deeds.*

In our culture, mystical experiences, when they are misunderstood, may drive individuals into therapy.

**Prof:** "To help you understand mystical thinking, please read this poem by Rumi, a Sufi mystic (1207-1273 A.D.)."

### Say Yes Quickly

Forget your life. *Say God is great.* Get up.
You think you know what time it is. It's time to pray.
You've carved so many little figurines, too many.
Don't knock on any random door like a beggar.
Reach your long hand out to another door, beyond where
you go on the street, the street
where everyone says "How are you?"
and no one says *How aren't you?*

Tomorrow you'll see what you've broken and torn tonight,
thrashing in the dark. Inside you
there's an artist you don't know about.
He's not interested in how things look different in moonlight.

If you are here unfaithfully with us,
you're causing terrible damage.
If you've opened your loving to God's love,
you're helping people you don't know
and have never seen.

Is what I say true? Say *yes* quickly,
if you know, if you've known it
from before the beginning of the universe.

*Films: Siddhartha; Moses; The Last Temptation of Christ; Jesus of Montreal; Therese; Brother Sun, Sister Moon; Gandhi; Close Encounters of the Third Kind; The Passion of Joan of Arc.*

# NARCISSISM

*A Greek myth: Narcissus, a handsome youth, falls in love with his own reflection in a pool of water and pines away until he dies. So narcissism is self-love, being stuck at an early phase of development where the object of affection is the self. A reaction to shame in childhood.*

As an adult, the narcissist remains totally absorbed his own concerns. Narcissistic, deadbeat fathers abandon their families, fail to pay child support, and condemn their wives and their children to poverty.

**Narcissist:** "I don't have enough for myself, let alone the ex-wife and kids. Let her go on welfare."

**Narcissist to clerk:** "Do you have a pair of sunglasses with mirrors on the inside of the lenses? That way I can always see how I look."

**Doctor:** "I've examined you very thoroughly and at great expense and can find nothing wrong with you."
**Narcissist:** "Keep looking."

**Friend:** "What cosmetic surgery are you having next?"
**Narcissist:** "I think I'll have my elbows done. I've already had a tummy and eyelid tuck, a buttocks and face lift, a new nose, chin, and cheekbones."

**Therapist** *(yawning)*: "I'm bored going over this same material again and again. You're still as self-absorbed as you ever were. Aren't you bored with yourself, too?"
**Narcissist:** "Never."
**Therapist:** "I don't feel we're getting anywhere, so I want to give you a referral to another therapist."

**Narcissist's theme song** *(sung to self in bathroom mirror)*: "I'm in love with you, honey...."

**Ex-husband of narcissist:** "She took everything but the blame."

*Films: Alfie; I, Claudius; Diary of a Mad Housewife; Portnoy's Complaint.* If you would be offended by a sexually explicit film, skip *Caligula* (the ultimate narcissist).

# OBSESSIONS

*Uncontrollable patterns of thought about anger, contamination, sex, hoarding, religion, or the need for symmetry. Repetitive, irrational behavior.*

Obsessions appear in the form of ideas that are unwelcome, unpleasant, and cause anxiety. For example, thoughts about death, toilet functions, sex acts, or mutilation of oneself.

**Client:** "I'm frantic. Every time I walk into the kitchen, I have the urge to put my hand in the garbage disposal."
**Therapist:** "I propose that we treat you with behavior modification techniques. You're involved with OCD–obsessive compulsive disorder."

**Priest** *(trained in Europe)*: "Americans are obsessed with sex, money, power, and spirit. These subjects are loaded because they're associated with sin, and no one wants to go to hell. Every person I meet in the States either feels enraged, guilty, or insecure about at least one of them."
**Parishioner:** "You just pressed all of my buttons!"

**Client:** "I haven't come to see you in anger. I've come in a fury! I'm obsessing about the teachers I trusted who said God was fair and life would be good."
**Therapist:** "They lied...."
**Client:** "What?"
**Therapist:** "Or it just may be that you don't know the end of the story yet."

**Woman** *(talking about a lover)*: "I'm going to get him away from his wife."
**Girlfriend:** "How do you propose to do that?"
**Woman:** "I'll be there every time he turns around. I think about him day and night. I've stopped sleeping. I may have to kill the wife to get her out of the way."
**Girlfriend:** "You're kidding, right?"
**Woman:** "I've never been more serious in my life."

*Films: The Mission, Of Human Bondage, Obsession, Ossessione, Jean De Florette, Claire's Knee, Fatal Attraction, Misery, The Collector, Bagdad Cafe, The Blue Angel, Dead Ringers, The Horse's Mouth.*

# OEDIPUS/ELECTRA COMPLEX

*The Greek myth: Oedipus is a tragic character who, due to a dire prophecy, is separated from his family at birth. Years later he returns to his homeland, ignorant of the identity of his real parents and, under bizarre circumstances, slays his father. He next meets the widow, his own mother, and marries her. When he discovers the horrible truth, he blinds himself.*

This classic tale–of the killing of a father by his son and the marriage of the son to his mother–provided Freud with a way to identify the substance of a common pattern, namely the incestuous fixation of a son upon his mother.

**Prof:** "We expect sons to love their mothers, but not to marry them. The normal man learns about loving womankind at his mother's side and transfers this love to another woman as he matures. He then marries and moves on to create his own family."
**Student:** "And if he gets stuck?"
**Prof:** "If he is unable to develop beyond infantile or adolescent focus on his mother, we say he is dominated by the Oedipus complex. For a challenging movie on the Oedipal issue, check out George C. Scott and his maturing son as they battle for mother in *The Savage Is Loose*."
**Student:** "What's the Electra complex?"
**Prof:** "It takes its name from another classic and tragic Greek myth, in which a young woman named Electra, in the bitter climax of the tale, kills her mother to avenge her father's death. So, 'Electra' is used to describe the father complex: excessive attachment to the father and hostility toward the mother."
**Student:** "Do parents have to be seductive with their children for these complexes to develop?"
**Prof:** "Usually, yes. There's a fine line between normal, healthy attachment of children to their parents and unhealthy fixation. Seductive parents say things like, 'When you grow up you'll never love anyone else as much as you do me,' rather than, 'When you grow up you'll find a mate you'll love as much as you do me.' "

**Comic:** "Oedipus, shmedipus, as long as you love your mother."

*Films: The Silver Cord, The Savage Is Loose, Oedipus Rex, Mourning Becomes Electra, Iphigenia.*

# PARANOID

*Clinical definition: a person afflicted with the mental disorder "paranoia" (or "paranoid schizophrenia"), which is characterized by delusions^ of persecution or grandeur, and hallucinations.^*
*Popular definition: those who feel others are plotting against them.*

An example of a delusion of grandeur is a madman who insists: "I am God" or "I am Jesus."

**Paranoid:** "People out there want to kill me. That's why I carry a gun."
**Therapist:** "Can you consider the possibility that this fear of people you believe want to hurt you is a projection of your own rage and of your own wish to hurt others?  And that you don't see it because such terrifying hostility is unacceptable to your conscious mind?"

**Hospitalized paranoid:** "They're out to radiate me. That's why I line all my clothes and hats with aluminum foil!"

**Divorcing wife:** "He had my tires slashed, my brake cables cut twice, and broke into the house to rig the clothes dryer so it would blow up. He's trying to kill me."
**Therapist:** "What do the police say?"
**Divorcing:** "They took a complete report and dusted the dryer for fingerprints. They could see how the gas pipes had been tampered with, but there is no conclusive evidence. I had to call the gas company to fix it. I'm frightened out of my wits."
**Therapist:** "You're not paranoid. You're right. He is trying to kill you. What other steps can you take to protect yourself until the police nail him?"

**Bumper stickers for paranoids:**
"If you can read this, you're an alien trying to steal my brain like you stole Elvis's."
"President of the World and Damn Proud of It."
"Guns Don't Kill people–I Do."

**Therapist joke:** Paranoia can occur in females, males, and those who have not yet decided.

*Films: Taxi Driver, Paranoia, Paranoiac, Nightmare on Elm Street.*

# PATHOLOGICAL LIAR

*A borderline person (one on the edge of psychosis^) who often cannot tell the difference between fact and fantasy, or who lies to achieve felonious ends.*

Clients lie to their therapists to make themselves more acceptable, because they want the approval they didn't get as children. My clients were, by and large, a very loveable pack of liars, and I was devoted to them. However, pathological lying is the product of a severe personality disorder and frequently supports criminal intention: robbery, swindling, or sadism and sexual conquest.

**Bigamist:** "You're the only woman I ever loved."

**Con man:** "This deal is almost too good to be true."

**Casanova:** "You can trust me."

**Sadist:** "Let me tie you to the bed. It will be thrilling, I promise you."

**Nathan Detroit:** "I'll marry you someday."
**Girlfriend** *(blowing her nose)***:** "You've been saying that for 14 years. After waiting around, never knowing whether it's on or whether it's off, a person could develop a cough...."

**Used-car salesman:** "One owner–a little old lady in Pasadena."

**Pool shark and hustler:** "I'm a beginner."

**Murderer:** "We'll just take a little walk down this path into the forest. There's something I want to show you."

**Rapist:** "I'm here to check the plumbing."
**Victim** *(opening the door)***:** "The building manager sent you? Do you always work this late?"

**Nymphomaniac:** "Of course I came."

*Films: A Place in the Sun, Choose Me, The Imposter, Raising Arizona, Nasty Habits, Chameleon Street, The Hustler, Room at the Top, Time To Kill, Wild at Heart, The Captain's Paradise, Hero.*

# PATTERNS

*Personal and collective behaviors that spring from unconscious inner sources and cause us to think and act automatically in response to specific triggers or circumstances.*

Sometimes we behave in ways that are dumbfounding to ourselves and others. Why? We can speculate that we are imprinted with, or are endowed with and carry, unconscious patterns or programs of personality and behavior. We recognize them in others and, if we pay attention, in ourselves.

**Prof:** "If you are normal, as you walk down a street and pass a person of the opposite sex, your psyche will vote, 'yes, a possible sex partner' or 'no.' You ordinarily don't know you do it; the decision is unconscious. The evaluation occurs as a result of pattern recognition somewhere in your psyche. You recognize a pattern in another person that feels familiar and you are either drawn toward it or repelled by it. For example, a pattern may be like or not like that of your mother and/or father."

**Student:** "So what we have learned to love or hate in childhood, we continue to love or hate as adults?"

**Prof:** "Yes. For example, in first marriages, we almost always marry either our mother or father. Adult children of alcoholics, even though they may not be alcoholics themselves, walk around wondering why they feel so much distress, and why they choose alcoholics or addicts for mates."

**Student:** "I understand genetic predisposition, such as the fact that children of parents who've had cancer have a higher likelihood of developing the disease. Is this like that?"

**Prof:** "We're not sure if the patterns are linked directly to genetics, but they seem to have that kind of power over us. Particularly in darkside^ patterns–from the murderous inclinations of serial killers to self-destructive patterns like taking up smoking again after years of abstinence–we see the power of patterns to influence our lives."

**Thrilled woman:** "You're just like my father."
**Man on the make:** "Did you love him a lot?"

*Films: Johnny Apollo, Los Olvidados, The Last Temptation of Christ, Jesus of Montreal, Man Facing Southeast, Tortilla Flats, The Last Outlaw, Lonesome Dove.*

# PERFECTIONISM

*Setting personal standards of achievement that are unattainable. A self-tyranny guaranteed to make life miserable and bring continual unhappiness.*

A perfectionist is struggling to please some inner slave-driver, usually one or both parents, whose demanding behavior has been directly learned or introjected (psychologically absorbed). Nothing completely satisfies perfectionists. They can find the slightest flaw in anything they do, driving themselves crazy in their determination to fix it. They apply these standards to others as well, becoming judgmental and rejecting.

**Client:** "I'm never satisfied with anything I do. I'm always falling short of my objectives. Things don't work out the way I planned."
**Therapist:** "As human beings, we have a dark, less-than-perfect side, so your ideal of perfect, snow-white living is impossible. Life is sloppy and full of surprises."
**Client:** "I suppose I could strive for excellence instead of perfection, and do so without being compulsive about it."
**Therapist:** "That's healthy. On those occasions when you do achieve the excellence you desire, you can celebrate instead of trashing yourself for not getting there sooner."

**Woman** *(age 22)*: "I'm depressed because I'm not a Bo Derek 10."
**Therapist:** "When I look at you, I see a beautiful woman. What do you see in the mirror?"
**Woman:** "Nothing that $10,000 worth of liposuction won't cure."
**Therapist:** "Please read Naomi Wolf's *The Beauty Myth*, because you sound like a victim of media-hype images of beauty that are destroying the self-concept of many women in America. In the meantime, tell me how you didn't please your father...."

**Husband:** "What a great dinner party! You prepared it all yourself and everyone complimented you on how terrific the meal was. Beautiful table, everything beautifully served. I'm so proud of you."
**Perfectionist wife:** "The rolls weren't hot enough."

*Films: Diary of a Mad Housewife, The Odd Couple, A New Leaf, Sleeping with the Enemy.*

# PERSONA, EGO, SHADOW

*Jung's three major aspects of human consciousness:^ Persona is your idealized self-image, how you prefer to see yourself. Ego represents all you consciously know about yourself and what you are. Shadow is your unknown dark side,^ the aspect you don't know about (unless you work hard to become very conscious) and usually don't want to know about.*

Jung broke with Freud over their different perceptions of the nature of consciousness.^ (See also: ID, EGO, SUPEREGO)

**Voice of the Persona:**
"Never losing my temper makes me superior."
"I'm a fabulous wife and mother."
"I have no faults whatsoever."
"Nobody does it better."
See: Liv Ullman role in *Persona*.

**Voice of the Ego:**
"What you see is what you get."
"God isn't finished with me yet."
"I'm all I've got."
"The older I get, the less I know for sure."
See: James Stewart role in *Mr. Smith Goes to Washington*.

**Voice of the Shadow:**
"Me, take pleasure in hurting someone else? No way."
"The dark side of motherhood is control? Nonsense."
"Plow my wife when I'm mad at her? Who me?"
See: Robert DeNiro role in *The Mission*.

**Client:** "What do you mean I have a shadow side I'm unable to see? If that's so, how can I ever know anything about it?"
**Therapist:** "Pay attention to your reactivity. Just point your finger at someone you don't like or that you disrespect, and as you tell me about how awful the person is, you'll be describing your shadow."
**Client:** "You mean what I react to in them is in me? That's revolting, disgusting, and I don't believe it."
**Therapist:** "Most people feel the same way when they confront their shadow for the first time. It's humbling, it's humiliating. It puts a pin into their inflated ego."

*Films: Never Cry Wolf; Antarctica; Out on a Limb; Brother Sun, Sister Moon; Husbands and Wives.*

# PERVERSION

*Distorted behavior. A non-typical or even pathological (sick) deviation from normal, particularly in sexual habits.*

Perverts, who are usually male, love pornography which includes children or violence against women (in sexually explicit movies, literature, magazines, photographs, or videos).

**Students:** "Give us examples of perverted sources of sexual gratification."
**Prof:** "*Pedophilia* means satisfaction comes through sexual contacts with children. Child-molesting. It's one of the major reasons for the kidnapping of children. Pedophiles lack the ego-strength to make it with an adult of the same or opposite sex.
"*Fetishism.* Sexual satisfaction comes from objects, like shoes, or some part of the body (like the feet) other than the genitals.
"*Transvestism.* Satisfaction comes from wearing the clothes of the opposite sex. Who do you think steals all that lingerie and underwear from clotheslines?
"*Transsexualism.* Gender identification with the opposite sex. This is how we get those great female impersonators and cross-dressers.
"*Exhibitionism.* Flashing one's genitals to an unsuspecting observer. A fast cure for this problem is to invite the flasher's entire family for a session, have him come in naked, show his genitals, and say, 'It's all right for me to be a man.' That will end it.
"*Voyeurism.* Secret observations of someone else's lovemaking or genitals. Peeping Toms. Voyeurs make those jerk-off phone calls to total strangers. Patrons of Japanese peepshows where men anonymously watch girls take baths, dress, and do such ordinary things as housework, are voyeurs.
"*Bestiality.* Satisfaction comes from contact with animals. Shepherds are infamous for sex with ewes. And then there are those woman-and-donkey shows in Mexico...."

**Man:** "I've fallen in love with my horse."
**Therapist:** "You do have a problem."
**Man:** "I'll say. The horse isn't Jewish."

*Films: Crimes of Passion; Lolita; Peeping Tom; Klute; sex, lies, and videotape.*

# PHOBIA

*A paralyzing, irrational, debilitating, morbid fear of some object or situation which fills the sufferer with anxiety and with the panic that another such attack will come at any moment.*

Panic attacks occur without warning. In the midst of an attack, phobics think they are either going to die or go crazy. If the problem is untreated, their lives have to be cleverly arranged to accommodate the phobia. Then there is the fear of being found out.

**Prof:** "Among the common phobias is agoraphobia. An inaccurate definition: 'fear of being outdoors, in open spaces.' A better definition: 'fear of the anxiety that can lead to panic,' to quote Mel Green in *Living Fear Free*. For agoraphobics, life can become very limited. 'My heart starts beating so fast. My whole body turns into a sweaty bundle of nerves and my legs turn to rubber. It's getting so bad, I can hardly go to visit my relatives. Just to be away from home for five or ten minutes is a battle....' "

**Student:** "What's acrophobia?"

**Prof:** "Fear of heights. The acrophobic person finds it difficult to climb a ladder or look over the edge of a balcony, let alone something like the edge of the Grand Canyon. A college student who managed to graduate never took any classes above the first floor. We know why."

**Student:** "And claustrophobia?"

**Prof:** "Fear of enclosed places, like elevators, cars, closets, stairwells. Forget buying a cemetery plot and coffin. Plan for cremation instead."

**Student:** "Mysophobia?"

**Prof:** "Fear of dirt, germs, smoke, smog inhalation. Ever seen someone in a restaurant wiping and wiping his silverware and glass before the meal is served or someone wearing white cotton work gloves in an inappropriate setting? Now you know."

**Woman:** "I have a fear of flying."

**Therapist:** "I'll treat your symptoms with behavior modification so you can get on an airplane immediately. And in subsequent sessions, if you want to, we can work on your sexual fears, because flying is a metaphor for sex."

*Films: Arachnophobia, Vertigo, High Anxiety, The Vanishing.*

# POST-TRAUMATIC STRESS

*Trauma, a severe shock to the body or mind, is usually followed by a stress reaction which may last for years. The stress reactions range from mild to severe, depending on the severity of the trauma.*

**Client:** "My car was struck from the right and now I'm leery and nervous whenever I'm driving. Everything that comes at me from the right side of my car makes me jump."

**Therapist:** "We'll use systematic desensitization to treat the traumatic memories so they will lose their impact. First, visualize the accident close up, then a few hundred yards away, and finally a quarter of a mile away, and keep repeating that distant view until you relax. If you ever think of the accident again, immediately see it a quarter of a mile away."

**Vietnam vet:** "Three years of fighting and killing traumatized me so much that nightmares and grief are haunting me."

**Therapist:** "By any chance are you religious?"

**Vet:** "I was born Catholic but I never go to Mass anymore."

**Therapist:** "You must have absolution. If you're not willing to have a priest do it, you'll have to let your patron saint give it to you. Do it in prayer. Or I'll teach you how to write a dialogue with your patron saint so you can ask for absolution and forgiveness from him."

**Booking officer** (*at police station*): "Soliciting again? How'd you ever become a hooker?"

**Prostitute:** "Don't worry about it. My father and my older brother used me for sex for so many years, I just walk around numb. I'll never be able to be anything else but a whore. Everything I earn goes up my nose anyway, because the pain I'm in never stops and cocaine gives me relief."

**Officer:** "We just finished a course on post-traumatic stress and its symptoms. You have all the signs, and ought to be treated by a therapist. Maybe you'd begin to heal the wounds left over from childhood and adolescence."

**Prostitute:** "Are you gonna pay for it?"

**Officer:** "I forgot you have no union and no insurance!"

*Films: Regarding Henry, The Prince of Tides, Another Part of the Forest, Jacob's Ladder, Rambo: First Blood, Awakenings.*

# PREJUDICE

*Negative bias. Pre-judging a person, situation, place, or group of people without evidence to support one's position. A corrosive kind of thinking with profound social implications.*

Because our relatives hate and fear selected others, we learn to do the same thing in childhood. Whatever racial, ethnic, religious, and gender conflicts they are living become part of us through the power and energy with which they share them. Their terror and their hatred become our terror and our hatred.

**Prof:** "Sad to say that those who are targets of prejudice internalize the attitudes of their oppressors and carry a great deal of self-loathing. Sometimes they handle it by expressing hostility toward their peers (ghetto violence). Sometimes they handle it with a painful sense of humor. Henny Youngman:
'Why is a Jewish divorce so expensive?
'Because it's worth it.
'Why do Jewish men die before their wives?
'Because they want to.' "

"Why can't a woman be more like a man?"–Professor Higgins

**Black man** (*to his friends at the door of a white whorehouse*): "C'mon in. They just don't want to go to school with us."

**Therapist:** "You're fifty-nine years old and you only want to date girls in their twenties?"
**Client:** "Yes. I'm prejudiced against women my own age."
**Therapist:** "How old was your mother when you were born?"

**Father:** "He has no class, no education, no prospects, and he comes from the wrong side of town."
**Daughter:** "But I'm in love!"
**Father:** "Why can't you just fall in love with a horse, like the guy on page 82!"

*Films: The Civil War, Imitation of Life, El Norte, South Pacific, The Front, Enemy Mine, Skin Game, Guilty by Suspicion, The Man in the Gray Flannel Suit, The Defiant Ones, A Soldier's Story, Easy Rider, Mississippi Burning, Kings Go Forth, The Jerk, The Man from Down Under, Watermelon Man.*

# PROJECTION (A DEFENSE)

*What we see in significant others–lovers, friends, business associates, doctors, lawyers, therapists, and all those who evoke strong feelings or reactions. They are the screens upon which we display our own inner ideals, prejudices, expectations, dark side.*

The person we fall in love with does not really exist. He or she is a convenient vehicle for our projections of what is loveable.

**Love-struck man:** "You're so like my mother."
**Fiancee:** "Now that I've met her, I would never have guessed we have anything in common. Besides loving you, that is."
**Man:** "It's the feelings I have when I'm around you. You're like her."
**Fiancee:** "Well, that's fine with me for the moment, but maybe someday you'll see the real me."

**Wife:** "When I married you I had no idea you were so much like my father. I just knew I adored you. You and he are from such different backgrounds, with different looks and coloring. But now I see powerful similarities!"
**Husband:** "Is it me or is it your father in me that you love?"
**Wife:** "Both. I can't separate the feelings."

**Woman:** "I always find myself fighting with my mentors."
**Therapist:** "What do they have in common?"
**Woman:** "I idealize them, and when I find out they're not going to take care of me the way I expected they would, I become enraged."
**Therapist:** "You project 'ideal father' on them and, like a child, you expect to be taken care of just the way your father took care of you. Were you mad at him, too?"
**Woman:** "I must have been, because this situation repeats over and over with different men...."

**Mother:** "You must suffer in math classes. I always did."
**Daughter:** "Hey, Mom! I'm having a great time in trig and I'm taking calculus next."
**Mother:** "Imagine that!"

*Films: The Enchanted Cottage, Carnal Knowledge, The Prime of Miss Jean Brodie, Who's Afraid of Virginia Woolf, Women in Love, I Want to Live!, Elmer Gantry, Room at the Top.*

# PSYCHOLOGY

*From the Greek "psyche" (the love of or principle of life, soul, mind, breath) and "-ology" (the study of). Thus, the study of the psyche.*

The field of psychology deals with soul and spirit (psychognosis), mental processes and activities (psychodynamics), research about and measurement of mental ability (psychometrics), treatment of painful mental disturbance (psychotherapy, psychoanalysis), physical problems that have emotional components (psychosomatics). Other specialties are: forensic (legal), physiological (body and mind relationship), social psychology (people in context), and the latest field, eco-psychology (people and ecology).

**Student:** "I'm going to be a psychology major. What are my career options?"
**Prof:** "Research, or laboratory-based psychology to study behavior, from running rats through mazes to testing human subjects on almost anything."
**Student:** "If I'm interested in children?"
**Prof:** "Specialize in developmental or clinical psychology. Decide what your orientation will be. Mine is transpersonal.^ Study predictable stages in the physical, mental, and moral aspects of human unfolding from birth to death, and concentrate on children."
**Student:** "What do organizational and industrial psychologists do?"
**Prof:** "Develop tests for prospective employees, to predict those who will succeed, or analyze such things as how a change of speed on the assembly line will impact workers. Management, marketing, packaging, and sales are in the province of industrial psychologists, who consult with designers, manufacturers, corporations, business."
**Student:** "Suppose I want to work in clinical psychology?"
**Prof:** "You'll focus on mental health and the delivery of psychotherapeutic services."
**Student:** "Is that the same as counseling psychology?"
**Prof:** "There is overlap. Counselors provide guidance at all stages of life, from kids trying to figure out a program of study to seniors planning retirement. Clinicians, however, do psychotherapy with people who consult them for relief from pain."

*Films: Taking Off, The Marriage of a Young Stockbroker, The Cobweb, The Mark, The Third Secret, Repulsion, Morgan!, Cul-De-Sac, The Prince of Tides.*

# PSYCHOSIS/NEUROSIS

*Psychosis: insane thought processes and behavior.*
*Neurosis: thought processes and behavior that handicap an individual.*

Psychotics, once identified, are hospitalized or incarcerated for their own protection and the safety of the community. A neurotic person can still function in society, often quite well.

**Student:** "How do people become psychotic?"
**Prof:** "Psychoses can be caused by genetically transmitted brain defects, be drug-induced, brought on by trauma, or precipitated by a disease like syphilis. Some people become psychotic over time due to psychological pain or physical torture."
**Student:** "How are psychotics identified?"
**Prof:** "By obvious aberrant or unusual behavior. But some are never found out until one day they climb up a tower, start shooting, and kill someone."

**Neurotic woman:** "I need help. I couldn't sleep, so my physician ordered sleeping pills. Now I'm afraid to stop taking them because if I miss a night, I feel rotten."
**Psychologist:** "You have two different problems. One is sleep disturbance, the other is chemical dependency. Tell me the history of your insomnia, then I'll decide if I want to refer you to a clinic that specializes in sleep disorders, or if you couldn't sleep because of anxiety, which means I can treat you. If I proceed, we'll work out a schedule of slow drug withdrawal and deal with the anxiety as it appears."
**Woman:** "Okay! When I was a little girl, I used to be afraid to let my hands or feet get close to the edge of the bed before I fell asleep because something horrible under the bed would get me."
**Psychologist:** "So you've had sleep problems since childhood...."

**Neurotic:** "I'm going to kill myself."
**Psychotic:** "I'm going to kill you."

*Films: Raise the Red Lantern, One Flew Over the Cuckoo's Nest, The Snake Pit, 'Night Must Fall, What About Bob?, The Sea Wolf, The Cat and the Canary, Harvey, King of Hearts, Persona, Interiors, The Sterile Cuckoo, Portnoy's Complaint, Unlawful Entry, Bedlam, La Femme Nikita, Experiment Perilous, Thunder Rock, Dead of Night, The Dark Mirror, Possessed, Taking Off, The Third Secret, The Cobweb.*

# PSYCHOTHERAPISTS

*State-licensed clinicians who treat people (individuals, couples, families, groups) suffering from psychological and/or physical pain.*

Therapists earn a living by delivering mental health services in public agencies, hospitals, or in private practice. They receive salaries or are paid directly by clients, insurance companies, or the government.

**Student:** "I'm thoroughly confused by the many different kinds of psychotherapists. Can you help me sort them out?"
**Prof:** "You can tell a lot by the initials after their names. A *psychiatrist* is a licensed doctor of medicine (M.D.), whose specialty is mental health.

"A *clinical psychologist* is licensed, earned a Doctor's degree (Ph.D.) from an accredited university, and, in California for example, has at least 4500 hours of supervised clinical practice.

"A *clinical social worker* is licensed, has earned at least a Master's degree (M.S.W.) from an accredited university, and has had supervised clinical practice. Could hold a Doctor's degree (D.S.W.) as well.

"Some states license *Marriage, Family, and Child Counselors* (M.F.C.C.). They have earned at least a Master's degree (M.A.) in marriage and family therapy from an accredited university, and have passed a state exam after at least 3000 hours of clinical practice.

"*Pastoral Counselors* are trained in theological schools. They may have earned a Bachelor's (B.A.), Master's (M.A.), or Doctor's (Ph.D.) degree. Their work base is a church, synagogue, or other religious institution. Does this help?"

**Friend:** "How can you stand listening to all that pain every day?"
**Therapist:** "We're trained to be with those who have fallen into the abyss but not to fall in there with them."

**Weary therapist:** "Some days the borderlines just want to chew on my ankles."

*Films: Promise Her Anything; Oh, Men! Oh, Women!; A Fine Madness; The Group; Mine Own Executioner; Spellbound; The Dark Mirror; Possessed; Captain Newman, M.D.; Pressure Point; House of Games; The Couch Trip.*

# PSYCHOTHERAPY

*Treatment to relieve psychological pain. Same goals as psychoanalysis^*
*but uses different techniques. Therapists work from a broad spectrum*
*of theoretical orientations.*

Over 250 kinds of therapy are being practiced today.

**Student:** "Describe some different kinds of therapy."
**Prof:** "Crisis intervention is short-term, three to six hours, of therapy to
rapidly restore a client to his or her former level of functioning."

> **Client** *(in session at Crisis Center)*: "My canary died and I feel like
> killing myself."
> **Therapist:** "Has anyone else you loved died?"
> **Client:** "Yes, my grandmother and grandfather, my dad, my best
> girlfriend. I never cried."
> **Therapist:** "Then what we have here is one loss after another
> without any real mourning. It's cumulative grief. The death of
> your canary was the last straw, but if you cry, cry, cry, you'll
> feel better."

**Prof:** "The length of therapy depends on the speed with which the client
can deal with deep issues. The deeper and older the wounds, the longer
the healing may take."

> **Anal:** "I want to clean out my house. It's full. I have narrow aisles
> between gigantic piles of stuff."
> **Therapist:** "And when you try to throw things away...?"
> **Anal:** "I have a panic attack. I can't breathe."
> **Therapist:** "This may take a while to heal. Sounds like an
> obsessive-compulsive disorder^ to me."

**Prof:** "In family therapy, the counselor insists on seeing all members of
the immediate family."

> **Mother** *(talking about a child who is the family's emotional*
> *garbage can)*: "Fix this kid. The rest of us are fine."
> **Therapist:** "Your family is a system. If there are changes in
> this child's behavior, there will be some unpredictable changes
> in everyone else's feelings and their comfort levels as well."
> **Mother:** "Say what?"

*Films: Equus, Life Upside Down, Quartet, Bigger Than Life, House of*
*Games, Family Life.*

# PSYCHOTHERAPY DERAILED

*The contract–verbal or written–between client and therapist is broken.*

Therapist/client agreements to work together are based on mutual respect, what pioneering therapist Carl Rogers called "unconditional positive regard," plus trust and truth.

**Student:** "Why would clients leave therapy abruptly?"
**Prof:** "The therapist might feel they're not getting anywhere together and refer the client to another therapist. Or therapy could become uncomfortable, with the client fleeing from the work that might be required. A client could run out of money or insurance, relocate, or the therapist could behave unethically."

**Non-orgasmic woman:** "I've never been able to have an orgasm. Is something wrong with me?"
**Ethical psychiatrist:** "Probably you just don't know how. Most women experience orgasm by stimulating their own clitoris, and you can learn to do it by masturbating, maybe with a vibrator the first time to provide intense stimulation. Buy one, settle down comfortably in your bed, protect your sensitive skin, perhaps with a silk handkerchief between yourself and the vibrator, then stimulate yourself."
**Woman:** "But when I feel a lot of tension there from intercourse or from masturbating, I always stop."
**Therapist:** "That's how it feels just before the orgasm. Keep going and don't be afraid. Orgasm will release the tension."

**Unethical psychiatrist:** "I'll show you how an orgasm feels. Take off your panties and lie on the couch. This will be good for you."
**Non-orgasmic woman** *(later)*: "Can I sue?"
**Lawyer:** "Yes. Seduction in the name of therapy has serious repercussions. Your trust and your body have been violated and that's malpractice. The therapist can also lose his license after a hearing by an Ethics Committee which reports to the State Licensing Board."

Or, a "flight to health" may occur if a client is afraid.
**Nervous:** "Now that we've talked for a couple of hours, I feel completely cured of all my problems. Goodbye."

*Films: Equus, Trapped in Silence, What About Bob?*

# PSYCHOTHERAPY, OTHER NOTABLES

*In addition to Freud ^ and Jung,^ each of whom had his own version of psychoanalysis,^ a number of other significant theorists and practitioners contributed to the development of psychotherapy.*

**Student:** "Who are the Neo-Freudians?"
**Prof:** "A group of fine thinkers who were critical of Freud for one reason or another and who published their dissatisfaction and gathered their own followers. They included Alfred Adler, Otto Rank, Karen Horney, Harry Stack Sullivan, and Eric Fromm."
**Student:** "What about the humanistic approach?"
**Prof:** "The work of R.D. Laing and Rollo May led to the rise of the humanistic or human potential movement of the 1960s. This dimension of psychotherapy begins with investigating the alienation^ of persons, rather than with disease or internal conflict. Carl Rogers' 'client-centered therapy' directs the therapist to disclose that he is on the same journey toward wholeness as the client. Traditional analysts would rarely do such a thing."
**Student:** "Who is Fritz Perls?"
**Prof:** "He created Gestalt therapy. Because he placed the body at the same level of significance as the mind in the healing process, Gestalt therapy is holistic."
**Student:** "So some therapists work on the body, too."
**Prof:** "Oh, yes. Bodywork began with Wilhelm Reich's bio-functional therapy. After a thorough grounding in psychoanalysis, Reich began to work on his patients' bodies to break through muscular armor. His student, Alexander Lowen, founded what he called 'bioenergetics therapy.' Others who have worked directly on the body as well as the mind are Arthur Janov, Moshe Feldenkrais, Ida Rolf, all the sex therapists since Masters and Johnson, and the inventors of biofeedback."
**Student:** "What's transpersonal psychotherapy?"
**Prof:** "Inclusive or holistic attention to spirit, mind, and body in some combination by using meditation, dialogue, and/or bodywork to break into new dimensions of consciousness. Outstanding people in the field are Brugh Joy, Jack Kornfield, Claudio Naranjo, Stan and Christina Grof, Roger Walsh, and Frances Vaughan. Ken Wilber is the most influential theorist and spokesperson."

*Films: Chattahoochie, House of Games, Equus, Life Upside Down, Quartet, Bigger Than Life, Family Life.* **For other films related to this topic, see lists on pages 87, 88, 89, 91.**

# PUELLA

*Latin for "young woman" (pronounced "poo-__ella__"). A woman so in love with her father that she idealizes him and all men and also rejects her own femininity. A father-complected woman.*

Puella women disdain, even loathe themselves for being women and not men. They are thus wounded at the core of their being. In everyday language, they are disrespectfully referred to as "fathers' daughters," because they model themselves after their fathers and achieve to please them. Favorite puella song: "My heart belongs to Daddy...."

**Boyfriend:** "I've been dating you for months and all you ever talk about is your father."
**Girlfriend:** "I wasn't aware of that. Are you jealous?"
**Boy:** "Who wouldn't be? You make him sound like some kind of national hero."
**Girl:** "He is."
**Boy:** "Maybe this is going to be too tough an act to follow."

**Therapist:** "You're complaining about your boyfriend again? What is it this time?"
**Client:** "If only he could be more like my father...."

**Friend:** "Why do you take the blame for everything that goes wrong in your marriage?"
**Wife:** "I'm not sure. I read a book about women who love too much. Maybe I'm one of them...."
**Friend:** "You certainly never criticize your husband."
**Wife:** "He's so much more important than I am."
**Friend:** "That's crazy talk."

**Girlfriend:** "What do you mean, you're dropping out of college to go home to take care of your father? Your mother is there, isn't she?"
**Puella:** "Yes, but he needs me now more than ever, since he had a heart attack."
**Friend:** "Of course you want to go home to see him, but quitting your studies...? Phooey!"

*Films: Daddy Long Legs, Resurrection, Alice Adams, Splendor in the Grass, Father Knows Best.*

# PUER

*Latin for "youth" (pronounced "poo-air"). A puer aeternus ("eternal youth") is a man whose mother still has a psychological grip on his testicles and never lets go, even after her death. A mother-complected man.*

The Little Prince is a well-known fictional puer. So is Peter Pan. Some puers are homosexuals.^ At the other end of the splay of possible results from mother-domination are Casanovas, who either devastate the opposite sex or turn out to be unable to make a commitment to any woman. If they are not too neurotic, they marry but their attachment is tenuous.

**Puer:** "I must have powerful, dominant women in my life, just like my mother."
**Woman therapist:** "She gave you a lot, didn't she? You're sensitive, artistic, a healer, creative, talented, highly intuitive, deeply spiritual."
**Puer:** "I'm also a great lover, because I understand what women want. I know how to please a woman."
**Therapist:** "What about the dark side? Some puers feel fury and hatred about their unconscious sexual attachment to mother."
**Puer:** "Well, my mother could get me to do anything."
**Therapist:** "Did you ever feel like killing her?"
**Puer:** "Frequently."

**Wife:** "He walked away one day without a backward glance after 15 years of marriage."
**Friend:** "You never had a warning?"
**Wife:** "No. He seemed completely devoted to me and the children."

**Therapist:** "Why have you never married?"
**Puer:** "I'd have been perfectly happy if I could have married my mother. There is no one like her."
**Therapist:** "Did she have any faults?"
**Puer:** "None that I know of."

**Frustrated wife:** "Can't you ever make a move or a decision without calling your mother?"
**Husband:** "No."

*Films: The Silver Cord, The Loved One, No Way to Treat a Lady.*

# RATIONALIZATION (A DEFENSE)

*A logical or reasonable explanation as a cover for unacceptable actions, feelings, or thoughts. Purpose: to protect the ego.*

If we are unable to stand the pain of truth, we often rationalize.

**Student:** "I flunked a test in school today."
**Father:** "Why?"
**Student:** "Well, Grandpa is sick and I'm worried about him. I forgot to take my lunch money. My belt was too tight. I woke up early and I was tired. My pen stopped working in the middle of the test...."
**Father:** "Did you study?"
**Student:** "No."

**Sophomore:** "I asked Mary to go to the homecoming dance with me but she already has a date."
**Roomie:** "How do you feel about it?"
**Sophomore:** "I don't really like her that much."

**Therapist:** "We've been working on your addictions for the past two months, and your commitment is to pay for what we do together. So why don't you have a check with you?"
**Client:** "I forgot it because my car broke down."
**Therapist:** "You're supposed to write the check before we begin and hand it to me as you come through the door. That way you can see how much money you're investing in the next hour and you'll be motivated to get results. So what's the real reason?"
**Client:** "I reluctantly admit I'm mad at you because I'm still overeating and smoking."
**Therapist:** "I'm your therapist, not your fairy godmother. The kinds of changes you want to make are painful. If you want to stop smoking, I'll talk you through the withdrawals every hour on the hour, one day at a time. I recommended that you join a weight management program, but you haven't gone to any meetings. You must take responsibility for your own life, and you have to pay me to work with you. That's our contract. Go to the ATM machine at the bank downstairs."
**Client:** "You are one tough cookie."

*Films: The Bridge on the River Kwai, Robinson Crusoe, Mr. and Mrs. Bridge.*

# REACTION FORMATION (A DEFENSE)

*Behaving in a way that is the opposite of what one feels. The real feelings are unacceptable and would cause shame or embarrassment if experienced.*

Reaction formation is a powerful defense against being humiliated by the truth about oneself.

**Dependent client:** "You're telling me that dependency is one of the issues I need to confront? How do you know that?"
**Therapist:** "You were a dependent child—only eight years old—when your mother was hospitalized. Out of necessity, you had to take care of yourself when you really needed to be cared for by your mother. This situation would have left you with a deep need to be taken care of."
**Dependent:** "And no one came on the scene."
**Therapist:** "Exactly. So you began to take care of others. Why do you think you chose nursing as a profession?"
**Dependent:** "I thought it was because I am a very loving person."
**Therapist:** "Of course you are. But one dark aspect of nursing is the longing to be taken care of yourself."
**Dependent:** "This explains why I've overworked and let myself be taken advantage of in many situations."

**Therapist:** "You still can't admit that you could be stupid or ignorant about anything at all, can you? You've been defending your weaknesses by inflating yourself through teaching others."
**Teacher:** "Of course I know I'm incompetent is some areas."
**Therapist:** "Incompetent? Instead of accepting yourself as a human being with some strengths and some limitations, you are ashamed of the weaknesses. You only want to think about what is enhancing to your ego and hide the rest. No wonder you're so tense."
**Teacher:** "Are you telling me the reason I became a teacher is that I am ashamed of my flaws?"
**Therapist:** "Not flaws. Merely lesser amounts of skill and ability in some areas."
**Teacher:** "You mean I'm driven by some perfectionist^ ideals to cover my shame about weakness?"
**Therapist:** "You're finally getting the idea...."

*Films: Trust, Splendor in the Grass, Places in the Heart, East of Eden.*

# RECOVERY

*The slow process through which an alcoholic or addict becomes abstinent and takes charge of his or her life.*

Overcoming the defense of denial is the first hurdle.

**Alcoholic in detox:** "If I don't have a drink I'll die."
**Doctor:** "If you do have a drink you'll die."
**Same recovering alcoholic** *(later, at an Alcoholics Anonymous meeting)*: "Now I know if I drink, I'll die."

**Abstinent overeater** *(on the phone to Overeaters Anonymous sponsor)*: "I'm calling to commit my three meals for today."
**Sponsor:** "How many days have you been abstinent?"
**Abstinent:** "Nine! No sugar, no fats, no chocolate."
**Sponsor:** "Good work! If at any time you feel you're going to lose it, phone me."
**Abstinent:** "Okay! I'm going to an OA meeting at noon."
**Sponsor:** "Great! There's a noble and wise part of yourself...you can call it your Higher Power...that will help you get through the day, one hour at a time."

**Doper in the hospital** *(first day)*: "Which is harder to give up, cocaine or cigarettes?"
**Doctor:** "You came here to give up both of them."
**Doper** *(second day)*: "I feel like killing myself."
**Day 3, 4, 5, 6, 7:** "Ditto."
**Day 8:** "I feel a little hungry today. I'll live."

**Instructor at traffic school:** "Eighty-five miles an hour? How many times have you been to traffic school?"
**Speedster:** "Six or seven...."
**Instructor:** "Read that sign out loud."
**Speedster:** " 'The greatest predictor of serious injury accidents is citations!' "
**Instructor:** "And you plan to take a few other people with you when you suicide? Get real!"
**Speedster:** "I swear I am never coming back here again!"

*Films: A Hatful of Rain, Monkey on My Back, Looking for Mr. Goodbar, The Panic in Needle Park, Lenny, The Bottom of the Bottle, Red Sky at Morning, A Tree Grows in Brooklyn, Clean and Sober.*

# REGRESSION (A DEFENSE)

*Going backward, returning to earlier and less mature kinds of behavior, usually due to excessive stress.*

Under great stress, we may regress and repeat the same behavior with our children that our parents used with us, despite the fact that we hated it.

**Husband:** "Why are you smacking Bobbie? He only spilled a bowl of cereal."
**Wife:** "I've had a tough day with the kids, my head aches, and my dad hit me when I spilled things."
**Husband:** "But didn't you complain that your dad's treatment was abusive? I don't want you to hit the kids for no good reason."

**New mom** *(to neighbor)*: "Since the baby came, Jaimie wants his bottle again, even though I weaned him months ago."
**Neighbor:** "He's feeling replaced by and jealous of the baby. Why not try letting him have a bottle for the next few weeks, especially when you're busy nursing and can't hold him yourself?"

**Girlfriend:** "If we have a fight, you stick out your lower lip like you're a kid. Do you have to do that whenever you can't have your own way?"
**Boyfriend:** "It worked with mother."
**Girlfriend:** "But it's not working with me. Grow up!"

**Husband:** "It's two months since you lost your job, and now you sleep all day. I'm tired of this. So what if your company laid off half their employees? Get up, make the bed, take a shower, and let's have dinner."
**Wife:** "You're right. I can't find a new job if I'm not out looking for one."

**Mother** *(to teenage daughter)*: "All I did was ask you to clean your room, and you're having a tantrum!"
**Frazzled:** "It must be all the pressure I feel since I decided to try out for cheerleader."
**Mother:** "Drink this orange juice then go lie down and listen to some soothing music on your Walkman. The mess can wait...."

*Films: Baby Doll, The Frisco Kid, The Never Ending Story, 1984, Regarding Henry.*

# RELATIONSHIP

*Interaction between yourself and others. One of the two most important sources of information about who and what you are. The other major source is work.*

The "significant others" in one's life are, first, family members and, later, friends, teachers, lovers, mates, employers, members of the community. Depending on the vitality and intensity of these relationships, the importance of their feedback in shaping our self-concept is profound. Any discussion of relationship must eventually also include a consideration of one's relationship with the Life Force, whether one's feelings about the Life Force are positive, negative, or indifferent.

**Man:** "I'm incredibly lonely. It's hard for me to admit that."
**Woman:** "Me, too. Are you the one I've been looking for?"
**Man:** "Oh, God, I hope so."
**Woman:** "Let's just take our time getting to know each other."

**Grieving man:** "I don't know how I'm going to survive. My father died last year and now my mother has inoperable cancer."
**Therapist:** "You must be in terrible pain. When you're faced with two major losses, one right after the other, it's hard to imagine that grief will ever end. Who can comfort you? You need the rest of your family to share your pain right now."
**Grieving:** "When I was growing up, I was taught never to show pain. My father wouldn't let me or my brothers cry."
**Therapist:** "No wonder men in our society die so young."

**Woman:** "The most important relationship I have is with God."
**Friend:** "What do you mean?"
**Woman:** "I feel I'm being breathed by the Life Force every minute of every day. And when I'm really deeply relaxed, I'm cradled in the arms of the Almighty."
**Friend:** "If that's the case, you'd never feel lonely even if you weren't in relationship with a man."

*Films: The Lost Honor of Katharina Blum, Life and Nothing But, Late Spring, Entre Nous, Knife in the Water, Ju Dou, High and Low, The Green Wall, The Garden of the Finzi-Continis, Gertrude, Every Man for Himself and God Against All, The King of Comedy, East of Eden, Annie Hall, Enchanted April.*

# REPRESSION (A DEFENSE)

*The process, carried on outside of one's awareness, of pushing unacceptable thoughts and experiences deep into the Unconscious^ so the immediate tension and anxiety they create is eased. But they're still there and can be a source of serious maladjustment.^*

One of the purposes of therapy is to make conscious that which has been repressed, so a person can handle ideas and emotions that once would have been difficult. Then, instead of spending energy to keep bandages on old psychic wounds, a person can use the same energy for creative endeavors.

**Compulsive overeater** *(amazed)*: "Kill my mother to get her out of the way so I could have Daddy all to myself? No, no!"
**Therapist:** "It's a very common wish of little girls. Your hatred for your mother, which you still have, may have begun with this typical kind of longing to get her out of the way so you could possess your father."
**Amazed:** "But to kill her?"
**Therapist:** "You were physically abused by her. You would have been terrified, traumatized, and enraged at the same time, yet you were completely dependent on her. These conflicting emotions were too much for a child to handle, so the aggressive emotions were repressed."
**Amazed:** "Overeating helps keep them repressed?"
**Therapist:** "That's a partial explanation of how your self-abuse began, but there's more...."

**Molested woman:** "Sexually aroused when my uncle stood me on the toilet seat and put his penis between my legs? But I was only six years old!"
**Therapist:** "Babies are sexually stimulated when their bottoms are cleaned. As soon as the diaper is removed, they feel their genitals, so sexual pleasure begins in infancy. Your uncle's stimulation of your genitals, even though you knew it was taboo, was pleasurable to you. Maybe you felt fear, pleasure, arousal, and shame for being aroused by a forbidden kind of touching–all at the same time. Such conflict leads to repression of the unacceptable parts of the experience. But you don't have to be ashamed anymore."

*Films: Love Letters, Rain, Trapped in Silence, Cape Fear, Psycho, Silence of the Lambs.*

# RESISTANCE

*Opposition. Smokescreens. A common occurrence in the course of psychotherapy.*

Resistance may occur when a therapist gets too close to uncomfortable material. A client may actively prevent it from coming into awareness, especially if it involves experiences or feelings that have been repressed^ (pushed down into the Unconscious^ because they are painful or dangerous to one's self-concept^).

**Therapist:** "You're having difficulty remembering if you were ever molested as a child."
**Client:** "I don't want to talk about that."
**Therapist:** "If there was no problem, why are you so uncomfortable with my question? You could have just said 'no' and we'd go on to a different subject."

**Client** (*on the telephone*): "I have to cancel my next appointment."
**Therapist:** "Something we talked about today frightened or disturbed you?"

**Therapist:** "Every time the subject of your father comes up, you start to stutter. Have you noticed?"
**Client:** "I feel a lot of tension when I think about him."
**Therapist:** "What is there about your relationship with him that's difficult for you to examine?"
**Client:** "Nothing. Let's talk about something else."

**Therapist:** "Last week we talked about your mother and how she's influenced your attitude toward your husband. But today you began by discussing your job. Are we through with the subject of your mother, your husband, and your marriage?"
**Client:** "This will be my last session. I'm stopping therapy."

**Client:** "You don't understand me."
**Therapist:** "I'm the tenth therapist you've seen. Your pattern is to tell your story and split. You seem to have a desire to keep being a martyr or a victim."
**Client:** "I don't know about that...."
**Therapist:** "Unless you're ready to get off the cross, therapy is pointless."

*Films: Far and Away, The Accidental Tourist, Nuts.*

# RESPONSIBILITY

*Moral, legal, or mental accountability.*

A responsible person is "response-able" in appropriate ways; is trustworthy.

**International tribunal:** "You Nazis killed millions of people in your concentration camp gas chambers."
**Eichmann:** "I was only following orders."

"The buck stops here." – President Harry Truman

**Apologetic wife:** "I backed into a parked car when I was pulling out of a space at the supermarket."
**Irritated husband:** "Did you damage our car?"
**Wife:** "No. But I made a small dent in the other car."
**Husband:** "Did anyone see you?"
**Wife:** "No. I left my name and phone on the windshield, though."
**Husband:** "Our insurance premiums will increase."
**Wife:** "I'm sorry, but it was my fault."

**Irate neighbor:** "Your dog just took a dump on my lawn!"
**Responsible:** "Sorry. I'll come over and clean it up."

**Young man:** "You were supposed to use birth control!"
**Girlfriend:** "It didn't work. But you're the only one I'm sleeping with, so it's your kid!"
**Young:** "I hope you don't think I'm going to marry you. Go get an abortion. It's not my problem. Goodbye."

**Ecologist:** "Who dumped these tons of toxic chemicals?"
**Guilty:** "Who knows?"

**Judge:** "Driving under the influence. Well?"
**Drunk:** "I only had one beer."

**Mother:** "Which one of you kids made this mess?"
**Kid One:** "Not me."
**Kid Two:** "Not me."
**Kid Three:** "The cat did it."

*Films: This Land Is Mine, 12 Angry Men, The Verdict, Matewan, When Harry Met Sally, Robin Hood, Batman, Superman, Local Hero.*

# RITE OF PASSAGE

*A ceremony that marks the passing from one stage of life to another, more advanced stage. The most important of these are the rituals^ – elaborate and terrifying in some tribal societies– that mark the end of childhood and the beginning of adulthood.*

In many parts of the world, specific rituals welcome teenage children into adult society. These rituals are largely missing in Western culture. We prolong adolescence, and our kids are confused about when they can claim adult status.

**Disappointed Bar Mitzvah boy:** "I thought after I read from the Torah I'd be treated like a man, but my mother is still telling me how to wipe my nose."

**Father:** "You're sixteen years old today. Let's go down to the Department of Motor Vehicles and get your driver's license."
**Son:** "Does this mean I'm a real man now?"

**Father:** "You're seventeen years old today. Let's go down to my favorite whorehouse."
**Son:** "Does this mean I'm a real man now?"

**Father:** "You're eighteen years old today. Let's go down to the City Hall and register you to vote."
**Son:** "Does this mean I'm a real man now?"

**Father:** "You're twenty-one years old today. Let's go down to the Lazy J Bar, and I'll buy you a drink."
**Son:** "Does this mean I'm a real man now?"

**Son:** "So when am I going to be a real man?"
**Father:** "When you join the Army."

**Mother:** "Menstruation means you can have babies."
**Daughter:** "I'm bleeding. Am I a real woman now?"

**Boy** *(pressuring 13-year-old girl)*: "If you let me have sex with you, I'll make you into real woman."

*Films: The Emerald Forest, The Last Picture Show, The Hitcher, Smooth Talk, Twist and Shout, That Was Then...This Is Now, Vincent, Snow White and the Seven Dwarfs, Clash of the Titans, The Story of Abraham Lincoln, Total Recall.*

# RITUAL

*Ceremonies to punctuate life. Rites of passage.^*

Human beings thrive on ritual celebrations. Among the individual and family events that call for ritual: birth, marriage, death,^ and their anniversaries; inheritance, vacation, relocation, retirement, loss, First Communion, Bar Mitzvah, baptism, graduation. Among the collective events calling for ritual: a nation's founding, war and peace, return of soldiers after war, births and deaths of leaders. When important events are not marked by ritual, the psyche is strangely dissatisfied and we sense that something is missing.

**Disappointed mother:** "You're just moving in together?"
**Daughter:** "He hasn't asked me to marry him."
**Mother:** "We always dreamed of making you a beautiful wedding. The whole family and all our friends would give you presents to get your household started. I can't even buy you a trousseau...."
**Daughter:** "Mom, a wedding would be for you, not me."
**Mother:** "That's not true and you may live to regret this. Choosing your mate is one of the most important decisions of your life. We ought to be celebrating. Instead, I feel like crying."

**Vietnam vet:** "I don't know what went wrong. I spent three years in hell over there, was wounded in action, and when I got home, instead of being glad to see me alive, people would spit on me."
**Father:** "Son, I'm sorry. I'm proud of you, but the country was ambivalent about the war. The only way to redeem the warrior archetype^ is to win or to die."

**Racist:** "Why celebrate Martin Luther King's birthday?"
**Neighbor:** "If you don't know, I can't tell you."

**Immigrant:** "What is Thanksgiving Day?"
**Nightschool teacher:** "A national holiday that began soon after the Pilgrims arrived in America in 1620. They thanked God for a good harvest and had a great feast, with Indians as guests."
**Immigrant:** "I understand gratitude for America."

*Films: Picnic, Ring of Fire, Woodstock, Moana of the South Seas, Meet Me at the Fair, Always for Pleasure, Moonstruck, The Blue Lagoon, The Graduate, 9 1/2 Weeks.*

# SADISM

*Originally referred to sexual pleasure that comes from hurting a partner during sex, but now includes all forms of pleasure derived from giving pain.*

Taking pleasure from someone else's pain is neurotic^ (unhealthy) and in some cases is psychotic^ (insane).

**Wife:** "I feel I'm being tortured when you make love to me so violently that it hurts. I can handle an occasional black and blue mark, but pinching, slapping, and biting me to the point that I'm suffering will never be acceptable to me."
**Husband:** "I get off by doing that."
**Wife:** "I'm beginning to realize that you're a sick man and you need therapy. I refuse to put up with this kind of treatment any longer. I'm leaving you."

**Confused daughter:** "I don't understand why my mother is always telling me she saw something wonderful for me in a store, then she comes home empty-handed. She's been doing it all my life."
**Therapist:** "It's psychological sadism, a very subtle kind of torture."

**Madman:** "I loved every moment of the killing I did."
**Judge:** "You will be confined to a prison for the criminally insane for the rest of your natural life."

**Boss:** "Just because I said something about a raise doesn't mean you are automatically going to get it."
**Secretary:** "But you outlined exactly how much work you wanted from me, and I've been doing it all year...."
**Boss:** "Keep it up and maybe next year...."
**Secretary** *(to herself)*: "Take this job and shove it!" *(Aloud)* "I'm giving you two weeks' notice."

**Doctor in emergency room:** "Last month your child was burned. Now it's a broken arm. What goes on in your house?"
**Neurotic mother:** "My husband beats the kid when he's frustrated."
**Doctor:** "I have to notify the authorities. This is child abuse."
**Mother** *(to herself)*: "Better the kid than me...."

*Films: Silence of the Lambs, Blue Velvet, Angel Heart, Dangerous Liaisons, Sleeping with the Enemy, The Krays.*

# SELF

*Your individual personality.  Your conscious awareness of your continuing identity, plus your Unconscious^ (archetypal^ knowledge of everything in the universe).*

Freudian definition: the self is composed of *id* (primordial, animal), *ego* (what you are that you know about), and *superego* (controlling critic). Jungian: the self is composed of *persona* (the way you prefer to see yourself), *ego* (what you are that you know about), and *shadow* (what you don't see and usually don't want to know about).  (See ID, EGO, SUPEREGO and PERSONA, EGO, SHADOW.)

Ordinary ways of talking about the self:
**Teenage girl:** "My breasts are getting so big, I feel *self*-conscious."
**Friend:** "Not to worry.  If you've got it, flaunt it."

**Annoyed father** *(watching two-year-old son have a tantrum)*: "You've just got to learn to have some *self*-control!"

**Therapist** *(to woman in love with married man)*: "If you think he's going to marry you, it's *self*-deception."

**Woman** *(to friend)*: "Bob and I want to get married, but I can't because I have to take care of my mother."
**Friend:** "That's pathetic *self*-denial."

**Principal:** "We teach reading, writing, math, geography, history, science, phys ed, and *self*-expression."
**Uptight taxpayer:** "What's *self*-expression?"
**Principal:** "Being able to enjoy art, music, dance, drama, poetry, creative writing...all the finer things of life."
**Uptight:** "Not with my tax money.  Stick to the basics."

**Fortyish woman:** "I was dialoguing with a wisdom figure in my journal when this beautiful voice began to sing inside me."
**Jungian analyst:** "You didn't know it, but you'd been waiting for that moment all your life. Your eternal Deep *Self* has surfaced and is sharing the wisdom of the ages."

*Films: Never Cry Wolf, Antarctica, The Miracle Worker (1962), Fried Green Tomatoes, The Last Wave, The Illustrated Man, Out on a Limb, Coming to America, The Great Imposter.*

# SELF-CONCEPT

*"Global self-concept" describes your feeling toward yourself as a whole. "Partial self-concept" is your feeling about the quality and quantity of abilities you have.*

The global self-concept, or attitude toward one's whole self, is formed very early in life, usually between ages four and seven. It can be assaulted or enhanced anywhere on the road to maturity, but the feelings from childhood usually stick.

**Negative six-year-old:** "My mommy ran away and left me. She doesn't love me. I am very unloveable, and I feel sad about myself. I can't be fixed."

**Positive six-year-old:** "My daddy and mommy love me. I'm loveable, and I feel good about myself."

Partial self-concepts are based on discoveries we make about ourselves and on feedback from significant others.

**Six-year-old:** "I can jump rope already. I run faster than any boy in my class. Good body."

**Six-year-old:** "I can't read. I'm dumb."

**Sixteen-year-old:** "Men turn their heads to look at me. I'm sexy."

**Sixteen-year-old:** "I don't get this damn geometry. I must be math stupid."

**Twenty-six-year-old:** "My wife always has orgasms. I'm a great lover."

**Thirty-six-year-old:** "My kids get A's in school. I'm a good parent."

**Forty-six-year-old:** "I'm reaching the top of the corporate heap. In business, I'm very successful."

**Fifty-six-year-old:** "Oi! None of my children married. Where did I go wrong?"

*Films: Cleopatra; I Am a Fugitive from a Chain Gang; I Know Why the Caged Bird Sings; I Heard the Owl Call My Name; The Mission; Working Girl; Gandhi; Mother Teresa; Brother Sun, Sister Moon.*

# SEXUALITY, BI-

*The object of one's erotic attention can be either sex.*

Second only to the drive for survival, the energy to reproduce the species, *libido*, is the most powerful force we will ever experience. So it is not surprising that arousal occurs with any potential source of pleasure, male or female. Most of us are bisexual and are unconscious of that fact.

**Woman:** "It's hard to talk about this. I've been happily married for years, but there's a woman at the office I'm very attracted to."
**Therapist:** "I understand why you're afraid. Most women can be aroused by a member of their own sex. This is perfectly normal. But they don't choose to act out these feelings. Men are not the only ones who admire a centerfold."
**Woman:** "Well, that's a relief."

**Man:** "I'm married, I love my wife and children, but I occasionally go to bathhouses to meet other men."
**Therapist:** "Have you had an AIDS test?"
**Man:** "No."
**Therapist:** "Why not? You've been putting your own life and your wife's in jeopardy."

**Husband** *(to marriage counselor)***:** "I feel insanely jealous. My wife wants to leave me for another woman, and I want to kill both of them."
**Deserting wife:** "I'm more in love with my girlfriend than I am with my husband. Insecure men always think they may not be able to please a woman sexually and they wonder if another woman could do it better. That isn't the case, though, because most women enjoy their husband's penis. But for me, it's different. He was always very rough and fell asleep without ever making sure I was satisfied. She's giving me the tenderness and intimacy I've been craving for years."
**Therapist:** "So what are you going to tell the children, and who'll have custody?"

*Films: The Fourth Man, Victor/Victoria, Charley's Aunt, Some Like It Hot, Tootsie, Truth or Dare, Turnabout,* any porno film on the subject.

# SEXUALITY, HETERO-

*The object of one's erotic attention is the opposite sex.*

As we mature, we transfer our erotic attention from the parent of the opposite sex to another adult: "I want a girl, just like the girl that married dear old Dad...."

Depending on parental responses to our infantile fumblings with our genitals, we learn either to enjoy or suppress sexual feelings. To get a quick fix on your parents' attitudes toward sex, image yourself in bed having passionate sex with someone you adore. See your parents standing on each side of the bed watching. Look at the expressions on their faces. Are they happy, congratulatory, celebrating your satisfaction, or disapproving, disgusted, forbidding?

Interest in sex begins with children's questions:
**Child:** "What's sex?"
**Mom** *(to herself)*: "One of life's few free pleasures."
**Mom** *(to the child)*: "Did you see the big daddy rabbit climb on the girl rabbit at nursery school? He gave her his seeds, and then she could have babies."
**Child:** "Did it hurt?"

**Client:** "Sex with my wife is boring after 20 years."
**Therapist:** "Does she actively participate?"
**Client:** "No. She's too inhibited even to have a massage. She gets undressed in the closet."
**Therapist:** "She's extremely modest or ashamed of her body. Try this, and I'd say the same thing to her if she came in: check out your own technique by reading a popular book on how to satisfy your partner sexually. If you're convinced you've done everything you can to arouse her and it doesn't improve things, tell her you love her but you're unhappy because you're tired of making love to her when she's passive. Say you want both of you to enroll in a Tantra workshop, where you can learn new approaches. If she won't do it, tell her you want to take a mistress. Some European men feel it's a necessity. The wife is the children's mother; the mistress is for fun. She'll be hurt, shocked, or enraged; and she'll either be motivated to improve your sex life or agree to your having a mistress."

***Films:*** *Two Moon Junction, Rape of Love, Belle de Jour, James Joyce's Women, Hardcore.*

# SEXUALITY, HOMO-

*The object of one's erotic attention is the same sex.*

Recent studies indicate some differences in the size of left and right brain hemispheres between exclusively homosexual men and the rest of the population. This news will lead to debunking prior theories about why individuals become homosexual. We'll also soon know about brain size and chemistry in homosexual women.

**Man:** "I always felt my interest in other boys was unusual and I was uncomfortable with it."
**Therapist:** "What happened?"
**Man:** "I left my home town at seventeen and moved to San Francisco to go to college. After a while, I identified a gay bar, went in, and let an older man pick me up and initiate me. I was both terrified and thrilled. I'm a high school teacher. I couldn't get a job if I were a known homosexual."
**Therapist:** "Have you ever made a pass at one of your students?"
**Man:** "Absolutely not. I wouldn't think of doing that."
**Therapist:** "Do your parents know why they have no grandchildren?"
**Man:** "They suspect, but I haven't told them. I feel this news would break my father's heart."
**Therapist:** "What about your own broken heart?"
**Man:** "That's why I'm here. I want help to make a stable, long-term relationship."

**Lesbian couple:** "We've been fighting a lot lately."
**Marriage counselor:** "How long have you been together?"
**Couple:** "Ten years. Do you have any experience treating homosexual couples?"
**Counselor:** "As a matter of fact, I don't. But what makes you think your relationship problems are any different from hetero couples'?"

**Man:** "I came from Atlanta to San Francisco to have sexual freedom and I wound up as a male prostitute."
**Crisis Clinic psychiatrist:** "Do you have AIDS?"
**Man:** "Yes, but it's too late to cry."

*Films: Kiss of the Spider Woman, Turnabout, The Killing of Sister George, Myra Breckenridge, I Want What I Want, The Bitter Tears of Petra Von Kant, La Cage Aux Folles.*

# SHAME

*A feeling reaction that ranges from mild embarrassment to complete mortification. Reflects an inner wound.*

Children internalize parents' and the world's negative judgments, and some part of them cringes with shame. Only love and acceptance fortify the child against the damage of shame. Some therapists view shame as "the master emotion," the unseen regulator of our emotional life.

**The self-talk of a person who has been shamed in childhood:** "I am stupid [or ugly, impotent, unmanly, unfeminine, phony, incompetent, grasping, boring, cheap, ignorant, clumsy, not good enough, unloveable]."

**Mother** *(yells at child she finds masturbating)*: "I'm ashamed of you!"
**Child:** "What did I do wrong?"
**Mother:** "You're touching yourself where I told you not to."

**Vitriolic racist:** "You Jews killed our savior."
**Confused Jewish child:** "I didn't do it. Besides, Jesus was Jewish, too. Can I do anything about it?"
**Vitriolic:** "Hate yourself the way I hate you."
**Jew:** "Will that make you happy?"

**Taunting white kids:** "You're dirty, dirty, dirty."
**African-American child:** "I had a bath this morning. Or do you mean the color of my skin?"

**Wealthy client:** "I feel shame about all the money I inherited from my father, because so many people are living in poverty."
**Therapist:** "Why not set up a charitable trust and use your money to help some of them?"

**Macho father** *(to eight-year-old son)*: "Shame on you for crying about a little thing like a broken arm."
**Nurse** *(to herself)*: "Is he for real?"

*Films: The Nasty Girl, The Prince of Tides, Nuts.*

# SIXTH SENSE

*Mysterious ability to know through hunches, dreams, intuitions, expanded awareness. Capacity to use nonordinary sources of information.*

Women's intuition is commonly recognized. Artists, inventors, visionary poets, religious prophets, and others demonstrate that both sexes use nonordinary sources of inspiration. Shamans, tribal healers, and a few medical doctors "read" the body. Hawaiian Kahunas read clouds. Other sensitives read cards, tea leaves, *I Ching* coins or yarrow sticks, Tarot cards, handwriting, sheep entrails, crystal balls, astrology charts. Experience shows the abilities can be developed. The average person is awestruck, uncomfortable, intimidated, or skeptical in the presence of someone who is genuinely intuitive or psychic. Gullible people are easily fleeced by pseudo-psychics and charlatans.

**Wife:** "Let me read you today's astrology forecast."
**Husband:** "You know I don't buy that crap."
**Wife:** "But it's you!"

**Man:** "I woke up in the middle of the night and knew something had happened to my father. When I called the next morning, I discovered he'd had a heart attack at 2 a.m."
**Buddy:** "How do you suppose you knew that?"
**Man:** "I don't have a clue. There's no rational explanation."

**Student:** "What kinds of psychic abilities are there?"
**Prof:** "Quite a few, including clairvoyance, or the apparent power to perceive objects that cannot be seen with the eyes; clairaudience, or hearing what cannot be discerned with the ears; telekinesis, or moving objects with the mind; precognition, or knowing ahead; aura-reading, or seeing energy fields around the body and sometimes plants; and healing with laying-on-of-hands."
**Student:** "And what has been discovered about them?"
**Prof:** "Most claims are quickly debunked. But parapsychological researchers have also produced some very convincing data. The jury is still out regarding exactly what is what."

*Films: Resurrection, The Night My Number Came Up, Dead of Night, The Man Who Could Work Miracles, Flesh and Fantasy, The Night Has Eyes, The Clairvoyant, It Happened Tomorrow, I Love a Mystery, Enchanted April.*

# SOCIALIZATION

*The process through which we are taught, first by our family and then by others, how to live in society.*

We all learn the language of our parents, who also teach us what to eat, where to go to the toilet, how to get along, and how to keep out of danger. We learn about the different roles men and women play in society, how men and women earn a living, and what belongs to us and our family. In America, a significant amount of this socialization is being conveyed to children via television.

**A Kansas City 16-year-old:** "This is a tough generation to grow up in. You can't even watch a movie on TV without hearing cuss words and seeing someone shoot someone. Even the cartoons have violence. There's drug language all over TV...."

After 48 relentless hours of graphic, televised riot violence in L.A., including beatings, willful property destruction, looting, robbery, 1300 incidents of arson, four dozen murders, and mob hysteria, a TV reporter interviewing a cursing rioter cautioned, "You'll have to control your language if you're going to be on television."

**Pleading woman** *(to social worker)***:** "My grandmother was on welfare, my mother was on welfare, and I want to be on welfare, too."

**Mother** *(to little boy)***:** "You may not feel your penis in front of grownups or other children. It makes them uncomfortable. Do that in the bathroom or in bed."

**Little boy** *(comes in sobbing with a badly skinned knee)***:** "It hurts."
**Father** *(afraid to raise a wimp)***:** "Oh, no it doesn't." (This is one way men lose touch with their real feelings.)

**Boy** *(pressuring 13-year-old girl)***:** "Now that they give us condoms at school, sex is okay. Let's get one on."

**Mother:** "...and don't forget to wipe your behind."

*Films: Sugar Cane Alley, Home and the World, Law and Order, High School, The Yearling, To Kill a Mockingbird, Rikisha-Man, The 400 Blows, Fanny and Alexander, Lean on Me, Zero for Conduct.*

# SPIRITUALITY

*The capacity for awe and wonder, for connectedness, wholeness, and humility in the face of the infinite universe. A core, vital, integral dimension of human consciousness.*

"Spirituality is the courage to look within and to trust," said Carl Jung, one of the few scientists of the past century who had no difficulty discussing spirit. He described it as irrepressible.

**Physicist:** "The reason I became a scientist is that I had an experience with the stars when I was about nine years old. At that moment of my life, I was so enthralled and awed and inspired, I wanted to embrace the universe. But it was I who was being embraced by what I can only describe now as the Life Force, or God. I forgot about that for fifty years. I only recently rediscovered what has been motivating me my entire life. I'm grateful I'm still alive to share it."
**Friend:** "Listening to you, I'm the one who feels stunned."

**Seeker:** "Sir, you are a Christian monk who's been living in a Hindu ashram for 50 years. What is your feeling about Christianity now?"
**Bede Griffith:** "If Christianity cannot recover its mystical roots and teach them, it should fold up its tent, close its doors, and go out of business. It has nothing to offer."

**Woman:** "When I was a child I saw fairies in the bottom of the garden and had conversations with them. I had an imaginary playmate and I could also talk with all the animals in my neighborhood. Then I made the mistake of telling my father, who frowned and said in a very stern voice that it was time to grow up. So I stopped seeing and talking, except in a conventional way."
**Therapist:** "Why bring this to me?"
**Woman:** "Because I now have children of my own and I want to preserve their natural innocence and openness."
**Therapist:** "We're living in a rational, scientifically oriented society, and if your children are to avoid being held up to ridicule, they cannot expose their inner life too openly. It makes them very vulnerable."
**Woman:** "What a dilemma!"

*Films: Siddhartha; Moses; The Last Temptation of Christ; Jesus of Montreal; Therese; Brother Sun, Sister Moon; Gandhi; Close Encounters of the Third Kind; The Passion of Joan of Arc.*

# STIGMA

*"The mark of Cain." A sign of shame or discredit. Visible features such as birth defects (considered by the ignorant to be stigmas) and being born illegitimate, a member of a racial or religious minority, or poor are still stigmatizing in the United States today. Many stigmas can be overcome.*

In dark periods of history, criminals were actually branded with a hot iron. Everyone in the community could see the criminal's scar and be wary. In Puritan society, a woman accused of adultery was made to wear a scarlet letter "A" sewn on her clothing.

**Woman with secret:** "I've always been afraid I'd go crazy like my mother did and wind up in a mental hospital. No one in the neighborhood ever talked openly about her. I felt stigmatized. I never ever wanted anyone to know she went mad."
**Therapist:** "Why not?"
**Woman:** "Maybe people would say her kids literally drove her crazy. But, according to my father, she was schizophrenic by the time I was born."
**Therapist:** "Then what are you ashamed of?"
**Woman:** "Bad seeds...."
**Therapist:** "Your genes may make you vulnerable to schizophrenia but do not automatically condemn you to developing schizophrenia during your lifetime. Onset usually comes in late adolescence or early adulthood. You're already 40 and have no symptoms."

**Young male:** "Can I ever live down the stigma of killing my buddy in an auto accident? I was stoned at the time."
**Therapist:** "Yes. You must forgive yourself, stay off dope, and drive so carefully for the rest of your life that you never hurt another person. You can be hard-working, a big brother to some kid who has no father, and show the community that the accident made you humble and very caring."

*Films: The Scarlet Letter, Imitation of Life, any version of The Phantom of the Opera, The Hunchback of Notre Dame, Annie's Coming Out, My Left Foot, Johnny Belinda, Elephant Man, Johnny Handsome, Show Boat, The Man in the Gray Flannel Suit.*

# SUBLIMATION (A DEFENSE)

*Using sexual energy (libido) for other purposes.*

Converting a fundamental drive into alternate forms of expression.

**Mother** *(to 33-year-old daughter)*: "You turned down Bob's proposal? Aren't you ever going to marry and have a family?"
**Daughter:** "No. I'm putting all my creative energy into having a great career instead."
**Mother:** "I don't understand women in your generation. Bringing in the next wave of human beings is the most important thing women can do. You'd have great children."

**Married man** *(looking wistfully after a woman who is sauntering by)*: "I can't have all the women who are attractive to me."
**Male neighbor:** "You could always try...."
**Married:** "Let's go drive a few golf balls."

**Husband:** "Why don't you want to have sex during your period?"
**Wife:** "It's too uncomfortable and too messy."
**Husband:** "I think I'll make myself a cup of coffee and go down to my workshop. See you later."

**Teenage boy:** "After two hours of basketball practice, I'm too tired to think about girls."
**Friend:** "I'm never too tired to think about them. I just don't have the energy to do anything about it after pounding up and down the court to the point of exhaustion. But in a couple of hours...."

**Friend:** "You're working 20 hours a day?"
**Entrepreneur:** "That's what it takes to start a new business...about 18 months to get into the black."
**Friend:** "And your wife is complaining?"
**Entrepreneur:** "Our sex life is gradually drying up."
**Friend:** "Workaholics accomplish miracles, but if you don't plan for a day off once a week, your health will suffer, too. That's what the Sabbath was for. Even God rested...."

**Freud's notion:** Leonardo da Vinci couldn't get money, women, and power, so he sublimated it all and painted the Mona Lisa.

*Films: The Color Purple; Far and Away; Private Benjamin; Ruben, Ruben; The Deer Hunter; Dr. Zhivago.*

# SUFFERING

*From a therapeutic point of view, the major source of suffering is loss and a failure to release the attendant emotional pain. Suffering is also built into a life of dire poverty or severe physical handicap.*

Pain is inherent in the human condition because loss is inevitable. A healthy reaction to loss is grief, and grief must experienced. The pain of grief, and not knowing how to release it, often drives people into therapy.

**Client:** "My husband has a recurrence of his cancer."
**Therapist:** "Oh, my! How do you center^ yourself?"
**Client:** "Well, I meditate^ daily and exercise regularly. I'm cheerful and positive around the house."
**Therapist:** "What have you told your daughter?"
**Client:** "The truth. That we don't know one way or the other."
**Therapist:** "And how does she seem to be handling it?"
**Client:** "Her grades are going to hell in a handbasket."
**Therapist:** "Grieving, anxious children cannot be expected to perform up to their regular standards. Better notify your child's teacher about the exact nature of your situation."

**Wife:** "My husband doesn't love me anymore."
**Therapist:** "How do you know?"
**Wife:** "He told me. I'm so hurt and so mad at him, I feel like killing myself!"
**Therapist:** "You're in terrible pain about this crisis. Threatening to suicide is the only card you have left to try to control the situation. And if you did suicide to get even, to hurt him as much as he's hurting you, you'd punish everyone who knows you, especially your children. For the rest of their lives they'd be wondering if there was anything they could have done to save you. Besides revenge, what else do you have to live for?"

**Battered:** "My husband beat me up again."
**Therapist:** "Why do you put up with it?"
**Battered:** "You mean I don't have to?"

*Films: Ordinary People, City of Joy, Steel Magnolias, The Bicycle Thief, Salaam Bombay!, Jacob's Ladder.*

# SYMPATHY/EMPATHY

*Sympathy: identifying with the emotions expressed by another person.*
*Empathy: compassionate, unconditional acceptance.*

When we say therapists have empathic understanding of their clients, we mean they can understand why a client is suffering. But they don't have to suffer with the clients in order to help them.

*Sympathy–***Girlfriend** *(with tears rolling down her face)*: "Your mother died? How sad. I feel like crying, too."
**Grieving:** "All your sorrow must be for one of your own losses, not mine. Who did you lose?"

*Sympathy–***African-American** *(ready to riot)*: "Rodney King is angry. I'm angry, too!"
**2nd African-American:** "Angry? You haven't seen angry yet! I'm making some Molotov cocktails. Let's kick some ass."

*Sympathy–***Jewish mother:** "So you had an accident? I'll make you some chicken soup and you'll feel better."
**Son:** "Mamma, chicken soup won't fix the rear end of my car."
**Mother:** "No, but it will make your own rear end feel better."

*Empathy–***Therapist:** "Your seventeen-year-old son was struck by a car and died? You must be suffering and in terrible pain."
**Mother:** "Yes, and it's all his sister's fault for taking him on that trip in the first place."
**Therapist:** "What? Blaming your surviving daughter? You're using anger to keep from feeling the pain."
**Mother:** "I'm so mad at my son for dying!"
**Therapist:** "You have every right to be angry. Life isn't fair, but anger is poisoning you. Feeling anger hurts less than feeling grief. You need to cry a river during the next few months. You have to feel it to move through it. You can cry with me, then go home, slip into a warm bed with a box of tissues, and let the river roll."

*Empathy–***Therapist:** "You failed the real estate license exam again? You must feel incredibly frustrated."
**Client:** "I feel like jumping up and down and screaming."
**Therapist:** "This should be good. Go ahead. Let me see you do it."

*Films: The Other Side of the Mountain, Tomorrow, Ship of Fools.*

# TRANSFERENCE

*Unconsciously projecting^ (transferring) feelings associated with fathers, mothers, and significant others onto a therapist.*

Clients treat a therapist the way they learned to treat their parents in childhood. These projections give the therapist a look at the patterns and attitudes that cause dysfunction. For example, a client may be repeatedly late for sessions, forget to bring a checkbook, or miss an appointment. This is often the result of defiant anger left over from the relationship with father or mother.

**Therapist:** "You're late for the third time! It's a form of hostility to authority. If you don't arrive on time, I start without you."
**Client** *(laughing)*: "It is childish, isn't it?"
**Therapist:** "No. It's passive aggressive. Instead of telling me about your anger or disappointment or whatever emotion is real, you repress the hostility then show it to me by arriving late. Be direct instead of hiding. Get here on time and tell me about your real feelings toward me and our work."

**Woman therapist** *(to male client)*: "I notice you came in with your shirt unbuttoned to the waist and you are fondling your chest hair in a very seductive way. If you are trying to seduce me, it won't work. Tell me about the relationship between you and your mother."
**Client** *(buttoning up)*: "Now that you mention it, Mom and I were both seductive with each other."

**Therapist:** "After a year of very hard work, you're insulting me and questioning my competence. Is this what you had to do to leave your parents? Become very angry and push them away?"
**Client:** "Good questions. Let me think about it."
**Therapist:** "When we conclude your therapy, we'll take about six weeks to say goodbye in a calm and peaceful way. This is known as the process of termination. It will bring up any feelings you have about loss or abandonment. But now I want to hear about your disappointment with me."
**Client:** "You asked for it!"

*Films: Taking Off, The Marriage of a Young Stockbroker, The Cobweb, The Mark, The Third Secret, Repulsion, Morgan!, Cul-De-Sac, The Prince of Tides.* ***For other films related to this topic, see lists on pages 88-91.***

# TRANSFERENCE, COUNTER-

*An emotional reaction triggered in the therapist because the work being done by the client evokes either current or old unfinished business in the therapist.*

Counter-transference may cause the therapist to lose his or her ability to be a clear mirror for the client. If a case is troublesome, a therapist will seek consultation from another experienced colleague to review it. Jung said counter-transference is mysterious, but that it is the true source of healing for both client and therapist.

**Woman therapist:** "I need a consultation! I'm furious! My client, age 56, hasn't had an erection for three years. He's failed every time he's taken a very young woman to bed. I have been working with him for six months to help him be more realistic...to find an age-appropriate partner who has compassion."
**Consultant:** "What's this fury of yours about?"
**Therapist:** "He met one of my former clients at a workshop I was teaching. She's 48 and she's had a mastectomy. I worked with her so she could be sexual even though she only has one breast. When she took him to bed, he was successful after three years of impotence. Then he came into his session with me to complain that he didn't want to see her again because she wouldn't take off her brassiere. She was ashamed of her scar and the artificial breast she wears. I was so angry I wanted to throw him out of the office."
**Consultant:** "Are you feeling hurt by his rejection of a vulnerable woman? Do you think that your work with her all went down the drain?"
**Therapist:** "Yes to the first question. No to the second."
**Consultant:** "So you feel that his rejection of this woman meant you hadn't been effective with him. Instead of going on working with him so he could develop compassion for her, you rejected him just as he was rejecting her."
**Therapist:** "That feels right. Now I can see what I need to do to continue his treatment. I wanted to strangle him and was stuck in my reactivity!"

*Films: Lovesick; Whispers in the Dark; Promise Her Anything; Oh, Men! Oh, Women!; A Fine Madness; The Group; Mine Own Executioner; Spellbound; The Dark Mirror; Possessed; Captain Newman, M.D.; Pressure Point; House of Games; The Couch Trip.* **For other films related to this topic, see lists on pages 87, 88, 90, 91.**

# TRANSFORMATION

*Spiritual meaning: seeing the light of God. Or baptism.*
*Popular meaning: a positive, outstanding change in a person's charac-*
*ter, inner perspective, values.*

Major life-changing personal transformations can be generated by
mystical^ experiences, profound dreams,^ or stunning events such as
life-threatening disease, clear "ah-ha" moments, spontaneous realiza-
tions, or Grace.^

**Crips:** "The L.A. riots brought us to where we're saying, 'Let's stop
killing each other.' "
**Bloods:** "We agree to a truce."
**Precinct Captain:** "What a transformation! Let's hope this lasts,
because it could mean an end to kids killing kids out of boredom."

**Man:** "Since I've been doing Zen Buddhist meditation, I'm calm and
centered. And my meditation practice is deepening almost daily. My
whole life has changed and my ex-wife even looks good to me."
**Friend:** "Now that's what I call a transformation!"

**Woman:** "I once had a visionary experience that changed my life.
It happened spontaneously. I saw myself flying through the air on a
horse and it touched down in front of two gigantic carved doors. I was
terrified that something would be waiting to kill me behind the doors.
Nevertheless, I said aloud, 'Open the doors.' They swung open and
nothing was there except two more doors of similar appearance.
Because nothing bad happened to me when the first pair opened, I felt
courageous enough to say, 'Open all the doors!' With that I flew
through space into a light so blinding it was unforgettable and indescrib-
able, like nothing I have ever seen before or since. I had the sense I was
merging with the light, that I am that light and always was, and that I
have nothing to be afraid of, now or ever."
**Friend:** "But you're still fighting addictions."
**Woman:** "I'm just not finished with my transformation."

*Films: Agnes of God; A Christmas Carol; Resurrection; Born on the*
*Fourth of July; Perfect Strangers; Tender Mercies; Coming Home;*
*Goodbye, Mr. Chips; Hair; Golden Earrings; Backtrack; Irezumi (Spirit*
*of Tattoo); Quackser Fortune Has a Cousin in the Bronx; Malcolm X.*

# TRANSFORMATION, TRIGGERED BY DREAMS

*Stunning dreams can precipitate personal transformation.*

**Male client:** "I'm very upset. I must be going crazy. This morning, just as I woke up, I had a dream that I was all covered with gunk from a cesspool. It was disgusting! Then I cleaned off my skin with fire, planted a tree in the woods, and was going to plant another one just before I woke up."
**Therapist:** "What part of the dream didn't you like?"
**Client:** "The first part."
**Therapist:** "When were you like that before...all covered with slime?"
**Client:** "Never!"
**Therapist:** "Oh, yes you were. When you were born. You're giving birth to some new part of yourself."

**Female client:** "I had a powerful dream. Dazzling full-color. I'm in the lobby of an art school, flirting with a handsome man who invites me to look around. He says he'll meet me back there later. Then, in one studio, I come upon a woman making a magnificent mask out of clay and covering it with brilliant, gorgeous Italian turquoise-and-gold glass mosaic tiles. She hands it to me. I take it in a clumsy way, though I don't damage it, then I hand it back. When I return to the lobby, he is waiting. We cuddle together on a little couch, very intimately.

"He says, 'I don't hear as well through my left ear as I do through my right.'

"Surprised, I say, 'I don't see as well through my left eye as I do through my right.'

"He says, 'Oh, I can help you with that.'

"He reaches under the couch, pulls out a lighter that flames, and holds the flame a couple of inches in front of my left eye. I look through the fire and am stunned to see a cobalt blue night sky, full of dancing animals made out of stars. It's the most beautiful thing I've ever seen in my life! Tears of joy stream down my face. Out of my mouth come the words, 'I'm an artist. I've always been an artist, and I have to paint!' "
**Therapist:** "And you changed your whole life because of this dream?"
**Client:** "Yes."

*Films: Dreams, Jacob's Ladder.*

# TRANSPERSONAL

*A branch of psychology concerned with the study of humanity's highest potential and with the recognition, understanding, and realization of transcendent states of consciousness. Transpersonal psychotherapy combines Western ideas about the conduct of therapy with Eastern traditions.*

Transpersonal psychotherapists value each person's individual life story, no matter where it leads. They work on consciousness itself, as well as on changing the contents of consciousness. They teach meditation, centering, the value of making a sacred space for oneself, and appropriate care for the body (diet, exercise, rest). They stress the impact of archetypes and transcendent patterns on one's life and encourage their clients to seek out new experiences which trigger shifts in perspective.

**Man:** "When I'm surfing, I have a feeling of awe and wonder at the universe...something I can't find a name for."
**Therapist:** "These transcendent moments are 'mystical' experiences. Do you feel connected with God?"
**Man:** "Not if you mean a big daddy in the sky! My connection feels as though it is with a powerful force that moves the galaxies and creates and creates endlessly. But I'm not religious! I left the church of my childhood years ago."
**Therapist:** "Mystical experiences may have little to do with going to church. They are more likely to reflect your becoming aware of the universal, spiritual part of your being."
**Man:** "Everybody has this part?"
**Therapist:** "Yes. It leads you to feelings of wholeness, oneness, connectedness, openness, and relationship with the Life Force."

A famous actress searched all her life for a wise teacher. One day as she sat by the edge of the Nile and was dazzled by the silver and gold diamonds of sunlight sparkling on the surface of the water, an inner voice said to her, "What you have been looking for is looking through your eyes."

*Films: Brother Sun, Sister Moon; Bernadette; Major Barbara; The Passion of Joan of Arc; Meetings with Remarkable Men; Siddhartha; The Reincarnation of Golden Lotus; Double Life of Veronique; Playing in the Fields of the Lord; The Reincarnation of Peter Proud; Back to the Future.*

# UNCONSCIOUS, THE

*An ocean of energy and potential just beneath the surface mind of an individual. The repository for all our experiences, programs, and patterns, the storage center for all our seed potentials that are waiting to germinate.*

The surface mind, ordinary ego,^ is usually unaware of the patterns that trigger repetitive behavior. Often people walk around saying things like, "Why did I do that?"...never realizing they are like marionettes, with patterns in the Unconscious that pull their strings. Part of the work^ of awakening to who and what we are is to become familiar with our patterns so we are not so helpless when they activate.

**Therapist:** "How may I serve you?"
**Woman:** "Something happened that really frightened me when I was a child. I'm afraid of all men."
**Therapist:** "We can try hypnosis to see if the Unconscious will send up the memories."

**Collector:** "Where do you get your ideas for paintings?"
**Artist:** "A good metaphor would be that I have a well inside me. I send down a bucket and it comes up full almost every time."

**Mathematician:** "I work like hell on a problem. Then I have to leave it alone. Often, while I'm doing something else, like taking a walk in the park, the solution appears. It's as if a part of me in the Unconscious has been working on it all the time."
**Colleague:** "I often see a solution just as I wake up in the morning."

**Client:** "I thought I was running my life! Now you tell me patterns in my Unconscious are doing it! Bah! Humbug!"
**Therapist:** "You're the one who married three times and now sees you married the same person each time! Your dreams and your reactivity to people will help make you conscious of these things. You may suffer when you first discover what your patterns are, but when you can accept all of yourself–your dark side as well as your incredible capacity for loving–you'll be whole."

*Films: Silence of the Lambs, Dracula (1931 version), The Damned, It's a Wonderful Life, My Fair Lady, Alice in Wonderland, Fantasia, Gene Autry and the Underground Empire, Citizen Kane, The Wolf Man.*

# UNCONSCIOUS, COLLECTIVE, THE

*"A vast sea or envelope of forces surrounding the earth."– Teilhard de Chardin.*
*"All the prior history and experiences of humanity. The archetypes^ that appear in myths and stories from all over the planet."– Carl Jung.*

Forces in the Collective Unconscious drive individuals as well as entire groups of people, from families to nations.

**Student:** "How do you explain the Nazi movement?"
**Philosopher:** "It was an eruption of the dark side out of the Collective Unconscious."
**Student:** "Awesome! But doesn't education play an important role in the development of national character, too?"
**Philosopher:** "If you mean that the German schools took wonderful children and turned them into idiots, that's certainly the case, but the forces beneath the surface were nevertheless archetypal.^ When you see a film such as *The Triumph of the Will* or German newsreels from the Hitler era, you can see the German people caught up in the expression of profoundly dark forces."
**Student:** "What's interesting to me is that these same German people, who invented 'the final solution,' generated some of the greatest classical music ever written."
**Philosopher:** "And so much of it...Beethoven, Bach, Hadyn, Brahms, Handel, Mozart, Richard Strauss. It staggers the imagination."
**Student:** "Genius must represent peaks in cycles of energy that move through the Collective Unconscious."

**Art Critic:** "What about an explosion of innovative art like the Impressionist movement in France? All those giants–Pisarro, Lautrec, Cezanne, Manet, Monet, Gauguin, Seurat, van Gogh–riding the crest of a wave of power out of the Collective Unconscious!"
**Naive:** "Maybe it was just a coincidence?"
**Critic:** "Get real!"

*Films: The Power of Myth* (Joseph Campbell with Bill Moyers, 6-part video*), 1984, Les Miserables, Joan of Arc, Something of Value, Triumph of the Will, War and Peace, The Civil War.*

# VICTIM CONSCIOUSNESS

*Being pitiful as a way to acquire a sense of personal power.*

What power? Victims use their power to manipulate others into feeling sorry for them, into taking care of them. Their helplessness, incompetence, and weakness tug at the heartstrings of those in a position to help them.

**Therapist:** "Only losers hang onto their treasured wounds and trot them out and milk them whenever it is convenient to do victim. They refuse to heal their wounds because they've become addicted to their own adrenalin. They will not forgive; they get off on suffering." ^
**Victim:** "I'm only telling you what happened...."
**Therapist:** "A martyr suffers in silence, but you are the kind of victim who won't let go of your suffering. You'll tell how it happened again and again and never stop because your suffering makes you feel special, even holy, like a saint."
**Victim** *(gnashing teeth)*: "I have to pay you to tell me this revolting news?"
**Therapist:** "If you don't want to go down without a struggle, at least get off the cross! There are too many people waiting in line. Your scar tissue will be stronger than your original flesh. Let's get busy with the healing!"

**Victim:** "It's all my mother's fault...."
**Therapist:** "We've done a great deal of work on this subject. She ruthlessly abused you, but when are you going to grow up and take charge of your life? That was then and this is now! You're still a prisoner of childhood. Are you ever going to make a prison break?"

**Man** *(to officer)*: "How can I avoid getting mugged in New York City?"
**Officer:** "Walk vigorously, with your head up and your chest out. Stride firmly. Look like you know where you're going and that you don't put up with nonsense. Unfortunately, this doesn't work for little old ladies, but you get the idea."

*Films: The Burning Bed, Sleeping with the Enemy, Mortal Thoughts, David Copperfield, Cape Fear, Shame.*

# VIOLENCE

*Any deliberate act involving physical force or the use of a weapon in an attempt to achieve a goal, further a cause, stop the action of another, defend oneself against attack, secure material reward, or intimidate others.*

My definition is from a study, commissioned by *TV Guide*, of the programs on ten television channels in Washington, D.C., on April 2, 1992, during the 18 hours from 6 a.m. to midnight. In all, there were "...1,849 individuals acts of violence, 175 scenes in which violence resulted in one or more fatalities, 389 scenes depicting serious assaults, 362 scenes involving gunplay, 673 depictings of punching, slapping, dragging, and other hostile acts, 226 scenes of menacing threats with a weapon."

**Margaret Mead** *(while criticizing American television for feeding so much violence into our collective consciousness, especially the minds of children, that we are racing toward passivity, and predicting that succeeding generations may become incapable of democratic thought)*: "I'm sick of being shocked!"

**Counselor** *(domestic violence specialist)*: "The court remanded you to therapy because you beat your wife and children so brutally that your wife wound up in the hospital."
**Macho man:** "She was asking for it."
**Counselor:** "Do you have any idea how you learned to recognize when someone is 'asking for it'?"
**Macho:** "The hard way. Grandpa beat my dad and Dad beat me."

**Rapist:** "The only way to get even with my mother and all women is to take one of them by force."

**Gang member:** "The only way to get into the hood is to kill somebody."
**Ambitious 12-year-old:** "Who?"
**Gang member:** "It doesn't matter."

**Horny husband to wife:** "Let's get violent!"
**Wife:** "As soon as I take a shower, I'll meet you in bed."

*Films: Boyz N The Hood, Ran, Power of One, The Killing Fields, American Me, Rambo (series), The Godfather, The Unforgiven, Friendly Persuasion, The Terminator, Terminator 2: Judgment Day, Streamers.*

# VISUALIZATION

*The use of images to augment traditional medical treatment and to achieve personal as well as communal goals.*

Visualization is an important aspect of human behavior. Healing images may arise spontaneously (in dreams or during meditation), intentionally (while following an exercise directed by a teacher, textbook, cassette tape, or videotape), or in daydreams.

**Student:** "How does imagery meditation work with cancer treatment?"
**Prof:** "Dr. O. Carl Simonton's empowering meditation uses guided imagery. During three 20-minute periods a day, patients imagine their white blood corpuscles mobilizing to destroy the cancer cells in their body. It's not a substitute for, but an addition to, chemotherapy, radiation, medication, or surgery."

**Trainer of therapists to class:** "You'll want to have an office that heals. Any images–whether they're paintings, photographs, drawings, prints, or posters–that are hung on the walls must communicate wholeness, peacefulness, serenity, centering, well-being, joy, beauty, bliss, calm. You can't overlook the importance of healing decor in psychotherapy, and you're modelling such an environment for your clients' homes, as well. You're all too young to remember how hospital rooms used to be sterile white, but research showed us that people didn't get well in them as fast as in rooms which are tastefully decorated."

**Basketball coach:** "Use creative visualization. Make pictures in your mind of hitting the basket. Use your imagination to make your hits concrete, and energy will flow to the images. It's not enough for you just to practice. You must also see yourself making baskets. No guarantees, but if you don't even have the basket clearly fixed in your mind, how can you hope to hit it?"

**Mother:** "I see you very successful, very fulfilled, very happy when you grow up."
**14-year-old:** "Do you see me making money?"

*Films: The Abyss, Alien, Aliens, Alien 3, Star Wars, The Dark Crystal, Fantasia, Beauty and the Beast* (Disney), *On a Clear Day You Can See Forever.*

# WORK

*Popular: labor to produce income.  One of the two most important sources of information about who and what we are (the other is relationship).*
*Psychological: internal process to develop and mature.*

"The work of the 90s is to clean up our inner houses."–Matthew Fox. By "inner houses," he means the personal (all the parts of us that are wounded and need healing) as well as the social (institutions, such as church, school, government, medicine).

**Monsieur Curie** *(grumbling)*: "Why do we have to boil these tons of pitchblende?"
**Madame Curie:** "Something there is calling me, and I must follow."
**Madame Curie** *(later)*: "Ah, this little trace is glowing in the dark. Let's name it radium."
**Monsieur Curie:** "Madame, I was mistaken.  You've discovered a new element.  The work was worth it."

**Floundering college student:** "I can't seem to find what my ideal work is.  I'm so caught up in my internal conflicts, I haven't had time to choose a major."
**Counselor:** "When you see yourself standing in a bookstore, what books are you looking at?"
**Student:** "Computer science, biology, sociology."
**Counselor:** "Your work will probably be in one of those fields.  Get videos out of the library that show careers in those areas and come back when you've had a look at them."

**Therapist:** "Why are you so driven?"
**Woman:** "Working eighty hours a week is too much?"
**Therapist:** "Do you love what you're doing?"
**Woman:** "Yes."
**Therapist:** "Then let's talk about balance in your life."

**Frustrated ghetto teenager:** "There isn't enough work to go around. I can't do anything but sell drugs."
**Officer on the beat:** "Soon you'll be on your way to prison."
**Frustrated:** "At least somebody will be taking care of me then."

*Films: Madame Curie, 9 to 5, Working Girl, Wall Street, The Freshman, Bugsy, Trading Places, The White Tower, Crossing Delancey, Jaques de Nantes, La Lectrice, City Slickers, On the Waterfront.*

# YOGA

*Hindu systems of physical and mental discipline designed to center consciousness and to reveal a union between the individual and Universal Mind. The ultimate objective of the practice of yoga is self-knowledge. In Sanskrit, yoga means "yoke," or "to join together."*

Hatha (body-oriented) yoga is widely taught in the U.S. today because it helps people to center in the midst of chaos and it provides stress-management skills. Usually presented as a form of exercise, yoga includes instruction in breathing, quieting the mind, and the slow and careful stretching of every muscle in the body to build physical strength and to calm and relax the body. The effectiveness of yoga improves with intense concentration.

**Student:** "How will I know I'm getting it?"
**Teacher:** "You'll see flashes of change once you begin to practice. As you learn to control your body, you'll gain confidence. As you begin to have times of greater tranquility, you'll know you are making progress."
**Student:** "I feel restless when I sit down to meditate."
**Teacher:** "You can learn to discipline your body to the point that it becomes quiet on demand. Exercise before you sit."

**Widow:** "My yoga is keeping me alive. I've been crying for months, but now I do my stretches instead."
**Friend:** "Will you show me what you're doing?"

**Teacher:** "I've been teaching yoga breathing in this prison for six months and I'll tell you this: you ex-addicts are doing terrific!"
**Con:** "I learned to hyperventilate and now I can get as high as I ever did on snow."
**Teacher:** "That's an unanticipated outcome, but if you've learned to turn yourself on by breathing, when you're released, you won't be driven to go back to your habit, and you won't have to steal."

**Student:** "Thank you for a wonderful class."
**Teacher:** "The test of a good teacher is how independent the students are after the instruction is over."

*Films: Gandhi, Down and Out in Beverly Hills, Always* (Jaglom version, 1985), *The Big Chill.*

# ZEST

*Enthusiasm for life.*

Zest is the enthusiasm people feel as they follow their bliss. It is a companion to the awe and wonder experienced by mystics, prophets, artists, poets, playwrights, and everyone involved in the creative process. It lures them ever onward and fills them with joy.

*Scene: two philosophers and two students seated around a table. The philosophers are responding to the students' questions.*
**Western philosopher:** "Your happiness and feelings of well-being and wholeness derive from your ability to move toward and eventually achieve your desired objectives."
**Eastern philosopher:** "Your happiness and feelings of well-being depend on learning to *be* rather than learning to *do*."
**Western student:** "I thought whoever dies with the most toys wins."
**Eastern student:** "I thought I was expected to enter a monastery, give up sex, and live a life of contemplation."
**Western philosopher:** "Neither of those positions is acceptable to most people. Happiness is about achieving balance. How you learn to center and balance your life is a function of your personal style and passion."
**Eastern philosopher:** "Love empowers my whole life. This is the most important thing I have to teach you. Love your work. Love other people. Love the Light within you. From these three sources, you'll get information about who and what you are."
**Western student:** "How can I find out more about who I am?"
**Eastern student:** "I want to know the same thing."
**Western philosopher:** "This is the most important question of your life. It's as if you're the Holy Grail itself and you're on a quest to find it."
**Eastern philosopher:** "This will be a most exciting journey. Actually, it's the only one worth taking."
**Eastern student:** "I do see there are no quick or easy answers."
**Western student:** "And the journey lasts a lifetime...."
**Philosophers:** "Yes, it does."
**Students:** "Thank you for sharing your wisdom."
**Philosophers:** "You're welcome. And now you're on your own."

*Film: Roger and Me, Reds, Patton, Personal Best, Norma Rae, Mephisto, Kagemusha, Hoosiers, Guilty by Suspicion, Not Without My Daughter, Inherit the Wind.*

# ALPHABETICAL LISTING OF FILMS

The films listed in this Appendix can be found at video stores, libraries, or in mail-order catalogues. Some films may be more difficult to locate than others. Be persistent. All were available at the time this book went to press.

# BIBLIOGRAPHY

GENERAL REFERENCE
Hill, G. *Illuminating Shadows: The Mythic Power of Film.* Shambhala. 1992.
Herink, R. *The Psychotherapy Handbook: The A to Z Guide to More Than 250 Different Therapies in Use Today.* NAL-Dutton. 1980.
Reber, A.S. *The Penguin Dictionary of Psychology.* Penguin. 1986.

ABUSE, OF SELF
Farberow, N.L. *The Many Faces of Suicide: Indirect Self-Destructive Behavior.* McGraw-Hill. 1979.
*The Twelve Steps of Overeaters Anonymous.* Overeaters Anonymous. 1990.
Wishnie, H. *The Impulsive Personality: Understanding People with Destructive Character Disorders.* Plenum. 1977.
Woodman, M. *The Owl Was a Baker's Daughter: Obesity, Anorexia Nervosa, and the Repressed Feminine.* Inner City. 1980.

ABUSE, OF OTHERS
Booth, L. *When God Becomes A Drug: Breaking the Chains of Religious Addiction & Abuse.* Tarcher. 1991.
Goffman, J.M. *Batterers Anonymous: Self-Help Counseling for Men Who Batter Women.* Batterers Anonymous. 1984.
———. *The Man Program: Self-Help Counseling for Child Molesters.* Batterers Anonymous. 1986.
Landau, E. *Child Abuse: An American Epidemic.* (rev.) J. Messner. 1990.
Pizzey, E. *Scream Quietly or the Neighbors Will Hear.* Enslow. 1978.
Walker, L. *The Battered Woman.* HarperCollins. 1980.

AGING
Andre, R. *Positive Solitude: A Practical Program for Mastering Loneliness and Achieving Self-Fulfillment.* HarperCollins. 1991.
Calyx Editorial Collective et al. *Women and Aging: An Anthology by Women.* Calyx Books. 1986.
Crook, T. and Cohen, G. (eds.) *Physician's Guide to the Diagnosis and Treatment of Depression in the Elderly.* Mark Powley Associates, Inc. 1983.
Ward, R.A. *The Aging Experience: An Introduction to Social Gerontology.* Harper & Row. 1984.

ALCOHOLISM
Al-Anon Family Group Headquarters, In Staff. *One Day at a Time in Al-anon.* Al-Anon. 1988.
*Alcoholics Anonymous, Third Edition.* Alcoholics Anonymous World Services, Inc. 1976.
Doris, M. *The Broken Cord.* HarperCollins. 1990.
*Twelve Steps and Twelve Traditions.* Alcoholics Anonymous World Services, Inc. 1978.
Woititz, J. *Adult Children of Alcoholics.* Health Communications, Inc. 1990.

ALIENATION

Bing, L. *Do or Die.* HarperCollins. 1992.

Dossey, L. *Recovering the Soul: A Scientific and Spiritual Search.* Bantam. 1989.

Frankl, V.E. *Man's Search for Meaning.* Pocket Books. 1984.


ANALYSIS, PSYCHOANALYSIS    See also FREUD and JUNG

Freud, S. *An Outline of Psychoanalysis.* Norton. 1949. Originally published in 1940.

———. *Introductory Lectures on Psychoanalysis.* in J. Strachey (Ed. and trans.) *The Standard Edition of the Complete Works of Sigmund Freud.* Vols. 15 and 16. Hogarth. 1961 and 1963.


ANGER, PERSONAL and COLLECTIVE

Frankel, L.P. *Women, Anger, and Depression: Strategies for Self-Empowerment.* Health Communications, Inc. 1991.

Tavris, C. *Anger: The Misunderstood Emotion.* Simon & Schuster. 1982, 1989.


ANXIETY

Jung, C.G. *Answer to Job.* Princeton U. Press. 1972.

Wholey, D. *Becoming Your Own Parent.* Doubleday. 1988.


APATHY

Macy, J. *Despair and Personal Power in the Nuclear Age.* New Society. 1983.


ARCHETYPES

Anderson, W. *The Green Man: The Archetype of Our Oneness with the Earth.* HarperSanFrancisco. 1990.

Campbell, J. with Moyers, B. *The Power of Myth.* Doubleday. 1988. Plus six hours of videotapes with the same title, which are classics.

Estes, C.P. *Women Who Run with Wolves: Myths and Stories of the Wild Woman Archetype.* Ballantine. 1992.

Houston, J. *The Hero and the Goddess: The Odyssey As Mystery and Initiation.* Ballantine. 1992.

Jung, C.G. *The Archetypes and the Collective Unconscious.* Princeton/Bollingen. 1968.

Moore, R. and D. Gillette. *King, Warrior, Magician, Lover: Rediscovering the Archetypes of the Mature Masculine.* HarperSanFrancisco. 1990.

———. *The King Within: Accessing the King in the Male Psyche.* William Morrow. 1992.

Neumann, E. *The Great Mother: An Analysis of the Archetype.* Bollingen Series XLVII. Princeton U. Press. 1964.

Perera, S. *Descent to the Goddess: A Way of Initiation for Women.* Inner City. 1981.

Qualls-Corbett, N. *The Sacred Prostitute: Eternal Aspect of the Feminine.* Inner City. 1988.


ASTONISHMENT

Fulghum, R. *All I Really Need to Know I Learned in Kindergarten: The Essay*

*That Became A Classic-With A Special Commentary.* Random House. 1990.

————. *Uh-Oh: Some Observations from Both Sides of the Refrigerator Door.* Villard. 1991.


BLAME

Ryan, W. *Blaming the Victim.* (rev.) Random House. 1976.


BOREDOM    See APATHY


BRAIN, RIGHT and LEFT

Edwards, B. *Drawing on the Right Side of the Brain.* St. Martin's. 1988.

Hatcher, M. *Centering Through Writing: Right Brain-Left Brain Techniques Applied to Writing.* U. Press of America. 1983.

Jaynes, J. *The Origin of Consciousness in the Breakdown of the Bicameral Mind.* Houghton-Mifflin. 1976, 1990.


BRAINWASHING

Aronson, E. *Age of Propaganda: The Everyday Use and Abuse of Persuasion.* W.H. Freeman. 1991.


CENTERING

Gendlin, E. *Focusing.* Bantam. 1981.

Hendrick, G. & Wills, R. *The Centering Book: Awareness Activities for Children and Adults to Relax the Body and Mind.* Prentice-Hall. 1989.

Pennington, M. *Centering Prayer: Renewing an Ancient Christian Prayer Form.* Doubleday. 1982.

Richards, M.C. *Centering in Poetry, Pottery, and the Person.* (2nd ed.) Wesleyan U. Press. 1989.

Sanders, L. *Centering: Your Guide to Inner Growth.* Inner Traditions. 1983.


CHILDREN

Hewlett, S. *When the Bough Breaks: The Cost of Neglecting Our Children.* Basic Books. 1991.

Plumez, J.H. *Successful Adoption: A Guide to Finding a Child and Raising a Family.* Harmony Books. 1982.

Youngs, B.B. *Stress in Children: Common Sense Advice on How to Spot & Deal with Stress in Children of All Ages.* Avon. 1986.


CO-DEPENDENCY

Beattie, M. *Codependent No More: How to Stop Controlling Others and Start Caring For Yourself.* HarperCollins. 1987.

Katz, S. & Liu, A. *Codependency Conspiracy: How to Break the Recovery Habit and Take Charge of Your Life.* Warner. 1991.

Schaef, A. *Co-dependence: Misunderstood-Mistreated.* HarperSanFrancisco. 1985.

Whitfield, C. *Co-dependence: Healing the Human Condition.* Health Communications. 1991.

## COMPASSION

Eppsteiner, F. *The Path of Compassion: Writings on Socially Engaged Buddhism.* Parallax Press. 1988.

Kohn, A. *The Brighter Side of Human Nature: Altruism and Empathy in Everyday Life.* Basic Books. 1990.

The Dalai Lama, *The Meaning of Life: From a Buddhist Perspective.* Wisdom. 1992.

## COMPULSION

Baer, L. *Getting Control: Overcoming Your Obessions and Compulsions.* Little. 1991.

Forward, S. *Obsessive Love.* Bantam. 1991.

Nakken, C. *The Addictive Personality: Understanding Compulsion in Our Lives.* HarperSanFrancisco. 1988.

Rapoport, J. *The Boy Who Couldn't Stop Washing: The Experience and Treatment of Obsessive-Compulsive Disorder.* NAL-Dutton. 1989.

## CONFLICT

Bramson, R. *Coping with Difficult People.* Dell. 1988.

Gillies, J. *Friends: The Power and Potential of the Company You Keep.* Coward, McCann & Geoghegan. 1976.

Needleman, J. *Money and the Meaning of Life.* Doubleday. 1991.

Robbins, A. *Unlimited Power.* Fawcett. 1987.

Rogers, C. *Carl Rogers on Personal Power.* Delacorte. 1978.

Wells, T. *Keeping Your Cool Under Fire: Communicating Non-Defensively.* McGraw-Hill. 1979.

## CONSCIOUSNESS

Chopra, D. *Unconditional Life: Mastering the Forces That Shape Personal Reality.* Bantam. 1991.

Progoff, I. *At a Journal Workshop: The Basic Text and Guide for Using the Intensive Journal Process.* (rev.) Tarcher. 1992.

## CREATIVITY

Goleman, D. et al. *The Creative Spirit.* Dutton. 1991. Companion to the PBS series.

Jampolsky, G.C. *One Person Can Make a Difference: Ordinary People Doing Extraordinary Things.* Bantam. 1990.

Leonard, L. *Witness to the Fire: Creativity and the Veil of Addiction.* Shambhala. 1990.

Torrance, E.P. *Guiding Creative Talent.* Prentice-Hall. 1962.

———. *Rewarding Creative Behavior: Experiments in Classroom Creativity.* Prentice-Hall. 1965.

## CRISIS

Grof, S. and Grof, C. (eds.) *Spiritual Emergency: When Personal Transformation Becomes a Crisis.* Tarcher. 1989.

## DARK SIDE

Bly, R. *A Little Book on the Human Shadow.* Harper & Row. 1988.

Joy, W.B. Avalanche: *Heretical Reflections on the Dark and the Light.* Ballantine. 1990.

Johnson, R.A. *Owning Your Own Shadow: Understanding the Dark Side of the Psyche.* HarperSanFrancisco. 1991.

Woodruff, P. & Wilmer, H.A. *Facing Evil: Light at the Core of Darkness.* Open Court. 1988.

Zweig, C. & Abrams, J. (eds.) *Meeting the Shadow: The Hidden Power of the Dark Side of Human Nature.* Tarcher. 1990.


## DEATH

Becker, E. *The Denial of Death.* The Free Press. 1973.

Kubler-Ross, E. *Death: The Final Stage of Growth.* Prentice-Hall. 1975.

————. *On Life after Death.* Celestial Arts. 1991.

————. *To Live Until We Say Good-Bye.* Prentice-Hall. 1980.


## DEFENSES, PERSONAL DEFENSES

Berne, E. *The Games People Play.* Ballantine. 1985.


## DEPENDENCY

Dowling, C. *The Cinderella Complex: Women's Hidden Fear of Independence.* Pocket Books. 1990.


## DEPRESSION (not GRIEF)

Burns, D.D. *Feeling Good: The New Mood Therapy.* Signet. 1981. Best self-treatment program for depression in the popular literature.

John-Roger and McWilliams, P. *Do It! Let's Get Off Our Buts.* Prelude Press. 1992.

Styron, W. *Darkness Visible: A Memoir of Madness.* Vintage. 1990.


## DISPLACEMENT

Firestone, R.W. & Catlett, J. *Psychological Defences in Everyday Life.* Human Sciences Press. 1989.


## DREAMS

Freud, S. *The Interpretation of Dreams. Basic Books.* 1955. First published in 1900.

LaBerge, S. *Lucid Dreaming.* Ballantine. 1986.

Lukeman, A. *What Your Dreams Can Teach You.* Llewellyn. 1990.

Taylor, J. *Dream Work: Techniques for Discovering the Creative Power of Dreams.* Paulist Press. 1983.


## DYSFUNCTIONAL (FAMILY, DEFENSES)

Fossum, M.A. & Mason, M.J. *Facing Shame: Families in Recovery.* W.W. Norton & Co. 1986.

Henry, J. *Pathways to Madness.* Random House. 1971.

Jerman, J. *Father-Daughter Incest.* Harvard U. Press. 1981.

## FAMILY

Adams, C. et al. *NO Is Not Enough: Helping Teenagers Avoid Sexual Assault.*
Impact. 1984.

Dyer, W.W. *What Do You Really Want For Your Children?* Avon. 1986.

Gordon, T. *P.E.T. Parent Effectiveness Training: The Tested New Way to
Raise Responsible Children.* Dutton. 1975.

Secunda, V. *Women and Their Fathers: The Sexual and Romantic Impact of
the First Man in Your Life.* Delacorte. 1992.

Schuller, A. *The Positive Family: Possibility Thinking in the Christian Home.*
Revell. 1983.

## FANTASY

Bettelheim, B. *The Uses of Enchantment: The Meaning and Importance of
Fairy Tales.* Vintage. 1989.

Bolen, J.S. *Ring of Power: The Abandoned Child, the Authoritarian Father,
and the Disempowered Feminine.* HarperSanFrancisco. 1992.

## FEAR

Beattie, M. *The Language of Letting Go: Daily Meditations for Codependents.*
HarperSanFrancisco. 1990.

Jampolsky, G.C. *Love Is Letting Go of Fear.* Celestial Arts. 1988.

Jeffers, S. *Feel the Fear and Do It Anyway.* Harcourt, Brace, Jovanovich. 1987.

## FEELINGS

Hillman, J. *Emotion: A Comprehensive Phenomenology of Theories and Their
Meanings for Therapy.* Northwestern U. Press. 1992.

Viscott, D. *Emotionally Free: Letting Go of the Past to Live in the Moment.*
Contemporary Books. 1992.

## FEMINISM

Faludi, S. *Backlash: The Undeclared War Against American Women.*
Crown. 1991.

Morgan, R. *Sisterhood Is Global: The First Anthology of Writings from the
International Women's Movement.* Anchor Press/Doubleday. 1984.

Smith, J.M. *Women and Doctors: A Physician's Explosive Account of Women's
Medical Treatment-and Mistreatment-in America Today.* Atlantic
Monthly Press. 1992.

Steinem, G. *Revolution from Within: A Book of Self-Esteem.* Little, Brown &
Co. 1992.

Tavris, C. *The Mismeasure of Women: Why Woman Are Not the Better Sex, the
Inferior Sex, or the Opposite Sex.* Simon & Schuster. 1992.

## FORGIVENESS

Jampolsky, G.C. et al. *Goodbye to Guilt: Releasing Fear Through Forgiveness.*
Bantam. 1985.

Simon, S.B. & Simon, S. *Forgiveness: How to Make Peace with Your Past and
Get On with Your Life.* Warner Books. 1990.

Smedes, L.B. *Forgive and Forget: Healing the Hurts We Don't Deserve.*
HarperSanFrancisco. 1991.

FREUD

Appignanesi, R. & Zarate, O. *Freud for Beginners.* Pantheon. 1979.

Badcock, C. *Essential Freud.* (2nd ed.) Blackwell. 1992.

Gay, P. (ed.) The Freud Reader. W.W. Norton. 1989.

Strachey, J. (ed.) *Standard Edition of the Complete Psychological Works of Sigmund Freud.* Hogarth Press. 1961-62-63.


GOD

Anderson, S.R. *The Feminine Face of God: The Unfolding of the Sacred.* Bantam. 1992.

Booth, L. *When God Becomes a Drug: Breaking the Chains of Religious Abuse.* Tarcher. 1991.

Campbell, J.*The Masks of God: Creative Mythology.* Penguin. 1970.

Fox, M. *The Coming of the Cosmic Christ.* Harper & Row. 1988.

————. *Original Blessing: A Primer in Creation Spirituality.* Bear & Co. 1983.

Kazantzakis, N. *The Saviors of God: Spiritual Exercises.* Simon & Schuster. 1969.

Suzuki, D.T. *An Introduction to Zen Buddhism.* Grove Press. 1987.


GRACE    See GOD


GRIEF (not DEPRESSION)    See also SYMPATHY

Colgrove, M. et al. *How to Survive the Loss of a Love.* Bantam/Prelude. 1976, 1991.

GUILT

Borysenko, J. *Guilt Is the Teacher, Love Is the Lesson: A Book to Heal You, Heart and Soul.* Warner Books. 1991.

Middleton-Moz, J. *Shame and Guilt: Masters of Disguise.* Health Communications. 1990.

Perera, S.B. *The Scapegoat Complex: Toward a Mythology of Shadow and Guilt.* Inner City Books. 1980.


HALLUCINATION    See also DELUSION

Siegel, R.K. *Fire in the Brain: Clinical Tales of Hallucination.* Dutton. 1992.


HEALING

Joy, W.B. *Joy's Way.* Tarcher. 1979.

Klein, A. *The Healing Power of Humor: Techniques for Getting Through Loss, Setbacks, Upsets, Disappointments, Difficulties, Trials, Tribulations, and All That Not-So-Funny Stuff.* Tarcher. 1989.

Mindess, H. *Laughter and Liberation: Developing Your Sense of Humor.* Nash. 1971.

Murphy, M. *The Future of the Body.* Tarcher. 1992.

Probstein, B. *Healing Now: A Personal Guide Through Challenging Times.* North Star. 1991.

Siegel, B.S. *Love, Medicine & Miracles: Lessons Learned about Self-Healing from a Surgeon's Experience with Exceptional Patients.* HarperCollins. 1990.

Simonton, O.C. *The Healing Journey.* Bantam. 1992.

## HOSTILITY SYNDROME
Tart, C.T. *Open Mind, Discriminating Mind: Reflections on Human Possibilities.* HarperSanFrancisco. 1992.

## ID, EGO, SUPEREGO    See FREUD

## INCEST
Bass, E. & Davis, L. *The Courage to Heal: A Guide for Women Survivors of Child Sexual Abuse.* Harper & Row. 1988.

Butler, S. *Conspiracy of Silence: The Trauma of Incest.* (updated) Volcano Press. 1985.

Carnes, P. *Out of the Shadows: Understanding Sexual Addiction.* CompCare. 1992.

Forward, S. & Buck, C. *The Betrayal of Innocence: Incest and Its Devastation.* (rev.) Penguin. 1988.

Lew, M. *Victims No Longer: Men Recovering from Incest and Other Childhood Sexual Abuse.* HarperCollins. 1990.

## INNER CHILD
Bradshaw, J. *Homecoming: Reclaiming and Championing Your Inner Child.* Bantam. 1990.

Paul, M. *Inner Bonding: Becoming a Loving Adult to Your Inner Child.* HarperSanFrancisco. 1992.

## INTELLIGENCE
Fussell, P. *BAD or, The Dumbing of America.* Summit. 1991.

Miller, A. *The Drama of the Gifted Child: The Search for the True Self.* Basic Books. 1983.

Sternberg, R.J. *The Triarchic Mind: A New Theory of Human Intelligence.* Penguin. 1989.

## JUNG, CARL GUSTAV
Campbell, J. (ed.) *The Portable Jung.* Penguin. 1976.

Hannah, B. *Jung: His Life and Work: A Biographical Memoir.* Shambhala. 1991.

Jung, C.G. *Man and His Symbols.* Dell. 1968.

————. *Memories, Dreams, Reflections.* Vintage. 1989.

————. *Modern Man in Search of a Soul.* Harcourt Brace, Jovanovich. 1955.

Read, H. et al (W.McGuire, Exec.Ed.) *The Collected Works of C.G. Jung.* Princeton U. Press. 20 volumes published between 1947 and 1991, with two supplements, Vol. A and B.

Storr, A. (ed.) *The Essential Jung.* Princeton U. Press. 1983.

Wilmer, H.A. *Practical Jung: Nuts and Bolts of Jungian Psychotherapy.* Chiron. 1987.

## LETTING GO
Colgrove, M. et al. *How to Survive the Loss of a Love.* (rev.) Prelude Press. 1990.

Jampolsky, G.C. *Love is Letting Go of Fear.* Celestial Arts. 1972.

LOVE

Buscaglia, L. *Living, Loving, & Learning*. Charles B. Slack. 1982.

Jampolsky, G.C. *Teach Only Love: The Seven Principles of Attitudinal Healing*. Bantam. 1984.

Peck, M.S. *The Road Less Traveled: A New Psychology of Love, Traditional Values, and Spiritual Growth*. Simon & Schuster. 1988.


MASOCHISM

Chancer, L.S. *Sadomasochism in Everyday Life: The Dynamics of Power and Powerlessness*. Rutgers U. Press. 1992.


MEDITATION

Goldstein, J. and Kornfield, J. *Seeking the Heart of Wisdom: The Path of Insight Meditation*. Shambhala. 1987.

Goleman, D. *The Meditative Mind: The Varieties of Meditative Experience*. Tarcher. 1988.

Joy, W.B. *Joy's Way*. Tarcher. 1979. For a list of meditation tapes contact: Brugh Joy, Inc., Box 730, Paulden, AZ. 86334-0730.

Levey, J. & Levey, M. *The Fine Arts of Relaxation, Concentration and Meditation: Ancient Skills for Modern Minds*. Wisdom. 1987.

Maisel, E. *Tai Chi for Health*. Prentice-Hall. 1963.


MENOPAUSE

Lark, S.M. *Menopause Self-Help Book*. Celestial Arts. 1990.

Taylor, D. and Sumrall, A. *Women of the 14th Moon: Writings on Menopause*. The Crossing Press. 1991.

Walker, B.G. *The Crone: Women of Age, Wisdom and Power*. HarperSanFrancisco. 1988.

Weaver, R. *The Wise Old Woman: A Study of Active Imagination*. Shambhala. 1991.


MULTIPLE PERSONALITY

Casey, J. The Flock: *The Autobiography of a Multiple Personality*. Knopf. 1991.


MYSTICISM

Ariel, D.S. *The Mystic Quest: An Introduction to Jewish Mysticism*. Aronson. 1992.

Jacobs, L. *Jewish Mystical Testimonies*. Schocken. 1987.

Moyne, J. and Barks, C. *Open Secret: Versions of Rumi*. Threshold. 1984.

Pagels, E. *The Gnostic Gospels*. Vintage. 1981.

Zahava, I. (ed.) *Hear the Silence: Stories of Myth, Magic, and Renewal*. Crossing. 1986.


NARCISSISM

Covitz, J. *Emotional Child Abuse: The Family Curse*. Sigo. 1986.

Jacoby, M. *Individuation & Narcissism: The Psychology of Self in Jung and Kohut*. Routledge. 1990.

OBSESSION     See COMPULSION

OEDIPUS COMPLEX/ELECTRA COMPLEX
Masson, J.M. *The Assault on Truth: Freud's Suppression of the Seduction Theory.* HarperCollins. 1992.
Miller, A. *Thou Shalt Not Be Aware: Society's Betrayal of the Child.* NAL-Dutton. 1986.

PARANOID
See any basic book on abnormal psychology.

PATHOLOGICAL LIAR
See any basic book on abnormal psychology.

PATTERNS     See also ARCHETYPES
Donovan, M.E. & Ryan, W.P. *Love Blocks: Breaking the Patterns That Undermine Relationships.* Viking Penguin. 1989.
Joy, W.B. *Avalanche: Heretical Reflections on the Dark and the Light.* Ballantine. 1990.

PERFECTIONISM
LeBoutillier, M. *Little Miss Perfect.* MAC Publishing. 1987.
Wolf, N. *The Beauty Myth: How Images of Beauty Are Used Against Women.* Doubleday Anchor. 1992.
Woodman, M. *Addiction to Perfection: The Still Unravished Bride.* Inner City. 1982.

PERSONA, EGO, SHADOW                    See JUNG, CARL GUSTAV

PERVERSION
Fortune, M.M. *Sexual Violence: The Unmentionable Sin: An Ethical and Pastoral Perspective.* Pilgrim Press, NY. 1983.
Griffin, S. *Pornography and Silence: Culture's Revolt Against Nature.* Harper & Row. 1981.
PHOBIA
Forgione, A. & Bauer, F. *Fearless Flying: The Complete Program for Relaxed Air Travel.* Houghton Mifflin. 1980.
Green, M.D. *Living Fear Free: Overcoming Agoraphobia-The Anxiety/Panic Syndrome.* Warner Books. 1987.

POST-TRAUMATIC STRESS
Beneke, T. *Men on Rape: What They Have to Say about Sexual Violence.* St. Martin's. 1983.
Benson, H. & Klipper, M.Z. *The Relaxation Response.* Avon Books. 1976.
Breznitz, S. *The Denial of Stress.* Int'l. U. Press. 1983.
Ledray, L.E. *Recovering from Rape.* Henry Holt & Co. 1986.
Selye, H. *The Stress of Life.* McGraw-Hill. 1978.
Terr, L. *Too Scared to Cry: Psychic Trauma in Childhood.* Harper & Row. 1990.

Wallerstein, J. & Blakeslee, S. *Second Chances: Men, Women & Children a Decade after Divorce.* Ticknor & Fields. 1989.

PREJUDICE
Pettigrew, T. et al. *Prejudice.* Harvard U. Press. 1982.

PROJECTION    See DISPLACEMENT

PSYCHOLOGY
Fox, W. *Toward a Transpersonal Ecology: Developing New Foundations for Environmentalism.* Shambhala. 1990.
Hardy, J. *Psychology with a Soul: Psychosynthesis in Evolutionary Context.* Penguin. 1990.
Hillman, J. *Re-Visioning Psychology.* Harper & Row. 1988.
Houston, J. *The Search for the Beloved: Journeys in Mythology and Sacred Psychology.* Tarcher. 1989.
James, W. *The Varieties of Religious Experience.* University Books. 1963.
Lajoie, D.H. & Shapiro, S.I. "Definitions of Transpersonal Psychology: The First Twenty-Three Years," *Journal of Transpersonal Psychology.* V. 24. 1992.
Wilber, K. *No Boundary: Eastern and Western Approaches to Personal Growth.* Shambhala. 1981.

PSYCHOSIS/NEUROSIS
Chesler, P. *Women and Madness.* Harcourt, Brace, Jovanovich. 1989.
Galton, L. *You May Not Need A Psychiatrist: How the Body Can Control the Mind.* Simon & Schuster. 1979.
Torrey, E.F. *Surviving Schizophrenia: A Family Manual.* Harper & Row. 1988.

PSYCHOTHERAPISTS
Bruckner-Gordon, F. & Gangi, B.K. *Making Therapy Work: Your Guide to Choosing, Using, and Ending Therapy.* Harper & Row. 1988.
Lerner, H.G. *Women in Therapy.* Harper & Row. 1989.

PSYCHOTHERAPY
Abt, L.E. & Stuart, I.R. *The Newer Therapies: A Source Book.* Van Nostrand Reinhold. 1982.
American Psychiatric Assoc. *Diagnostic & Statistical Manual of Mental Disorders DSM III-R.* (3rd ed. rev.) A.P.A. Press. 1980. (Under rev. 4th ed.).
Engler, J. & Goleman, D. *The Consumer's Guide to Psychotherapy.* Simon & Schuster. 1992.
Herink, R. *The Psychotherapy Handbook: The A to Z Guide to More Than 250 Different Therapies in Use Today.* NAL-Dutton. 1980.
Hillman, J. & Ventura, M. *We've Had A Hundred Years of Psychotherapy and the World's Getting Worse.* HarperCollins. 1992.
Kahn, M. *Between Therapist and Client: The New Relationship.* W.H. Freeman. 1991.
Vaughan, F. *The Inward Arc: Healing and Wholeness in Psychotherapy and Spirituality.* Shambhala. 1986.

163

Wilber, K. *No Boundary: Eastern and Western Approaches to Personal Growth.* Shambhala. 1981.

## PSYCHOTHERAPY, OTHER NOTABLES

Green, E. & Green, A. *Beyond Biofeedback.* Knoll. 1989.

Minuchin, S. *Families & Family Therapy.* Harvard U. Press. 1974.

Satir, V.M. *Conjoint Family Therapy.* (rev.) Science & Behavioral Books. 1967.

Weeks, G.R. & L'Abate, L. *Paradoxical Psychotherapy: Theory and Technique with Individuals, Couples, Families.* Brunner-Mazel. 1982.

## PUELLA

Leonard, L. *The Wounded Woman: Healing the Father-Daughter Relationship.* Shambhala. 1983.

Secunda, V. *Women and Their Fathers: The Sexual and Romantic Impact of the First Man in Your Life.* Delacorte. 1992.

Woodman, M. *The Ravaged Bridegroom: Masculinity in Women.* Inner City. 1990.

## PUER

Kiley, D. *The Peter Pan Syndrome: Men Who Have Never Grown Up.* Avon Books. 1983.

————. *The Wendy Dilemma: When Women Stop Mothering Their Men.* Avon. 1985.

Lee, J. *The Flying Boy: Healing the Wounded Man.* (2nd ed.) New Men's Press. 1987.

Trachtenberg, P. *The Casanova Complex: Compulsive Lovers and Their Women.* Pocket Books. 1989.

von Franz, M.L. *Puer Aeternus.* (2nd ed.) Sigo. 1981.

RATIONALIZATION    See DISPLACEMENT

REACTION FORMATION    See DISPLACEMENT

## RECOVERY

Bradshaw, J. *Bradshaw On: Healing the Same That Binds You.* Health Communications. 1988.

Carnes, P. *A Gentle Path Through the Twelve Steps: A Guidebook for All People in the Process of Recovery.* CompCare. 1989.

Fossom, M.A. *Catching Fire: Men Coming Alive in Recovery.* HarperCollins. 1989.

Fossom, M.A. & Mason, M.J. *Facing Shame: Families in Recovery.* W.W. Norton. 1989.

Friends in Recovery Staff. *The Twelve Steps for Christians from Addictive and Other Dysfunctional Families.* Recovery. 1988.

Peele, S. et al. *The Truth about Addiction and Recovery.* Simon & Schuster. 1992.

REGRESSION    See DISPLACEMENT

RELATIONSHIP

Bertine, E. *Close Relationships: Family, Friends, Marriage.* Inner City. 1992.

Goffman, E. *Interaction Ritual: Essays in Face-to-Face Behavior.* Pantheon. 1982.

Johnson, R.A. *We: Understanding the Psychology of Romantic Love.* HarperSanFrancisco. 1985.

Stone, H. & Winkelman, S. *Embracing Each Other: Relationship as Teacher, Healer & Guide.* New World. 1989.


REPRESSION

Wolinsky, S. & Ryan, M.O. *Trances People Live: Healing Approaches in Quantum Psychology.* Bramble. 1991.


RESENTMENT

Stark, A. *Because I Said So: Childhood Dynamics and Office Politics.* Pharos Books. 1992.


RESISTANCE    See THERAPY


RESPONSIBILITY

Viscott, D. *The Viscott Method.* Pocket Books. 1990.


RITES OF PASSAGE

Scarf, M. *Unfinished Business: Pressure Points in the Lives of Women.* Doubleday. 1980.

Sheehy, G. *Passages.* Bantam. 1984.


RITUAL

Campbell, J. with Moyers, B. *The Power of Myth.* Doubleday. 1988. Plus six hours of videotapes with the same title, which are classics.

Cohen, D. *The Circle of Life: Pictures from the Human Family Album.* HarperSanFrancisco. 1991.


SADISM    See MASOCHISM


SELF

Bradshaw, J. *Bradshaw On: The Family: A Revolutionary Way of Self-Discovery.* Health Communications. 1988.

Chopra, D. *Perfect Health: The Complete Mind-Body Guide.* Harmony. 1991.

Gergen, K. *The Saturated Self: Dilemmas of Indentity in Contemporary Life.* BasicBooks. 1991.

Goffman, E. *The Presentation of Self in Everyday Life.* Doubleday. 1974.

Grof, S. *The Adventure of Self-Discovery: Dimensions of Consciousness and New Perspectives in Psychotherapy and Inner Exploration.* State U. of N.Y. 1988.

Hall, E.T. *The Silent Language.* Doubleday. 1973.

Josselson, R. *Finding Herself: Pathways to Identity Development in Women.* Jossey-Bass. 1987.

Stone, H. & Winkelman, S. *Embracing Ourselves: The Voice Dialogue Manual.* New World. 1991.

## SELF-CONCEPT

Almaas, A.H. *The Pearl Beyond Price: Integration of Personality into Being-An Object Relations Approach.* Diamond Books. 1988.

Belenky, M.F. *Women's Ways of Knowing: The Development of Self, Voice, and Mind.* Basic Books. 1988.

Downing, C. *Mirrors of the Self: Archetypal Images Shape Your Life.* Tarcher. 1991.

## SEXUALITY, HETERO-, BI-, HOMO-

Barbach, L. *For Yourself: The Fulfillment of Female Sexuality.* Anchor Press. 1976.

Feuerstein, G. *Sacred Sexuality: Living the Vision of the Erotic Spirit.* Tarcher. 1992.

Laqueur, T. *Making Sex: Body and Gender from the Greeks to Freud.* Harvard U. Press. 1990.

McCloskey, J. *Your Sexual Health.* Elephas Books. 1992.

Symons, D. *The Evolution of Human Sexuality.* Oxford U. Press. 1979.

Zilbergeld, B. *The New Male Sexuality.* Bantam. 1992.

## SHAME

Bradshaw, J. *Healing the Shame That Binds You.* Health Communications, Inc. 1988.

Karen, R. "Shame," *The Atlantic Monthly.* Vol. 269 No. 2, February, 1992, pp. 40-70.

Middleton-Moz, J. *Shame and Guilt: Masters of Disguise.* Health Communications. 1990.

## SIXTH SENSE

Keyes, Jr., K. *Handbook to Higher Consciousness.* DeVorss. 1979.

## SOCIALIZATION

Henry, J. *Pathways to Madness.* Random House. 1965, 1971.

Pearce, J.C. *The Magical Child: Rediscovering Nature's Plan for Our Children.* NAL-Dutton. 1992.

———. *The Magical Child Matures.* Bantam. 1986.

## SPIRITUALITY     See also GOD, MYSTICISM, TRANSPERSONAL

Tarnas, R. *The Passion of the Western Mind: Understanding the Ideas That Have Shaped Our World View.* Harmony. 1991.

## STIGMA

Goffman, E. *Stigma: Notes on the Management of Spoiled Identity.* Publishers' House. 1963.

McEvoy, A.W. & Brookings, J.D. *If She Is Raped: A Book for Husbands, Fathers, and Male Friends.* Learning. 1984.

## SUBLIMATION     See DISPLACEMENT

SUFFERING

Eliot, R.S. and Breo, D.L. *Is It Worth Dying For? A Self-Assessment Program to Make Stress Work for You Not Against You.* (rev.) Bantam. 1989.

Fromm, E. *The Anatomy of Human Destructiveness.* Holt. 1992.


SYMPATHY/EMPATHY

Zunin, L.M. & Zunin, H. *The Art of Condolence: What to Write, What to Say, What to Do at a Time of Loss.* HarperCollins. 1991.


TRANSFERENCE and COUNTER TRANSFERENCE

Guggenbuhl-Craig, A. *Power in the Helping Professions.* Spring. 1971, 1990.


TRANSFORMATION

Gerzon, M. *Coming into our Own: Understanding Adult Metamorphosis.* Delacorte. 1992.

Woodman, M. *The Pregnant Virgin: A Process of Psychological Transformation.* Inner City. 1985.


TRANSPERSONAL

de Chardin, T. *The Phenomenon of Man.* HarperCollins. 1975.

Wilber, K. *No Boundary: Eastern and Western Approaches to Personal Growth.* Shambhala. 1981.

————. *A Sociable God: A Brief Introduction to a Transcendental Sociology.* McGraw-Hill. 1983.

Xavier, N.S. *The Two Faces of Religion: A Psychiatrist's View.* Portals Press. 1987.


UNCONSCIOUS, COLLECTIVE UNCONSCIOUS

Frey-Rohn, L. *From Freud to Jung: A Comparative Study of the Psychology of the Unconscious.* Shambhala. 1990.

Gellert, M. *The Still Good Hand of God: The Magic and Mystery of the Unconscious Mind.* Nicholas-Hays, Inc. 1991.

Jung, C.G. *The Psychology of the Unconscious.* Princeton U. Press. 1992.


VICTIM CONSCIOUSNESS

Baldwin, M. *Beyond Victim: You Can Overcome Childhood Abuse...Even Sexual Abuse!* Rainbow. 1988.

Bass, E. & Davis, L. *The Courage to Heal: A Guide for Women Survivors of Child Sexual Abuse.* Harper & Row. 1988.

Gawain, S. *Reflections in the Light: Daily Thoughts and Meditations.* New World. 1988.

Hay, L.L. *You Can Heal Your Life.* Hay House. 1988.

Hazelden Foundation, *Keep It Simple: Daily Meditations for Twelve Step Beginnings and Renewal.* HarperCollins. 1989.

Ryan, W. *Blaming the Victim.* (rev.) Random House. 1976.


VIOLENCE

Gelles, R.J. & Straus, M.A. *Intimate Violence: The Causes and Consequences of Abuse in the American Family.* Touchstone. 1989.

Miedzian, M. *Boys Will Be Boys: Breaking the Link Between Masculinity and Violence.* Anchor. 1992.

Miller, A. *For Your Own Good: Hidden Cruelty in Child-Rearing and the Roots of Violence.* (rev.) Noonday Press. 1990.

Moorehead, C. (ed.) *Betrayal: A Report on Violence Toward Children in Today's World.* Doubleday. 1990.

VISUALIZATION

Achterberg, J. & Lawlis, G.F. *Imagery and Disease: A Diagnostic Tool for Behavioral Medicine.* Inst. for Personality & Ability Testing. 1984.

Bry, A. & Blair, M. *Visualization: Directing the Movies of Your Mind.* Harper & Row. 1979.

Gawain, S. *Creative Visualization.* Bantam. 1983.

Samuels, M. & Samuels, N. *Seeing with the Mind's Eye.* Random House. 1975.

Simonton, O.C. et al. *Getting Well Again.* Bantam. 1982.

WORK

Beck, J. *Everyday Zen: Love and Work.* HarperCollins. 1989.

Dail, H. *The Lotus and the Pool: How to Create Your Own Career.* (rev.) Shambhala. 1989.

YOGA

Narashima, Swami B.V. *Self-Realization: The Life and Teachings of Sri Ramana Maharshi.* T.N. Venkataraman. 1985.

Prabhavananda, Swami & Isherwood, C. (trans.) *How to Know God: The Yoga Aphorisms of Patanjali.* New American Library. 1969.

Prabhavananda, Swami (trans.) *The Song of God: Bhagavad-Gita.* NAL-Dutton. 1989.

ZEST

Moore, T. *Care of the Soul: A Guide for Cultivating Depth and Sacredness in Everyday Life.* HarperCollins. 1992.

# About the Author

Frances Heussenstamm, Ph.D., is a Clinical Psychologist. She received her doctorate from the University of Southern California in 1968 for research exploring the relationship between creativity and alienation in adolescence. She has been a professor at both Columbia University, New York; and at California State University, Los Angeles; and she has been a Senior Research Associate at UCLA's Center for the Study of Evaluation and at the Center for Policy Research in New York. Dr. Heussenstamm took her clinical training at Mt. Sinai Hospital, Los Angeles, and maintained a private practice in Santa Monica, California, for a decade. She has trained teachers and other psychologists as well as members of the Peace Corps and Teacher Corps, and she has been a consultant to the U.S. Office of Education and many state agencies. Over 12,000 people have taken her psychology/journal workshops at UCLA and other universities; she has also taught those techniques in West Africa, Thailand, Australia, New Zealand, and India.